Bush Basics

BUSH BASICS

A Common Sense Guide
to Backwoods Adventure

GLEN STEDHAM

with illustrations by JILL DEULING

ORCA BOOK PUBLISHERS

Canadian Cataloguing in Publication Data
Stedham, Glen, 1944–
Bush basics

Includes bibliographical references and index.
ISBN 1-55143-098-3

1. Outdoors life. 2. Wilderness survival. I. Title.

GV200.5.S73 1997   796.5   C97–910424–6

Library of Congress Catalog Card Number: 97-68864

Cover design by Jim Brennan
Interior illustrations by Jill Deuling
Printed and bound in Canada

Orca Book Publishers   Orca Book Publishers
PO Box 5626, Station B   PO Box 468
Victoria, BC Canada   Custer, WA   USA
V8R 6S4   98240-0468

97 98 99   5 4 3 2 1

This book is dedicated to my wife Sherilyn, who puts up with my comings and goings and who proofread the manuscript. And to my daughter, Laura, with the hope that she will experience the pleasures of hiking during her lifetime as I have.

Allons! whoever you are come travel with me!

Traveling with me you find what never tires.

The earth never tires,

The earth is rude, silent, incomprehensible at first, Nature is rude and incomprehensible at first,

Be not discouraged, keep on, there are divine things well envelop'd,

I swear to you there are divine things more beautiful than words can tell.

> — *Song of the Open Road*
> Walt Whitman (1819 - 1892)

TABLE OF CONTENTS

ACKNOWLEDGMENTS

I would like to thank a number of people who contributed greatly to this project.

Professor Belton of Simon Fraser Univerity's Centre for Pest Management directed me to the appropriate sources and reviewed the final draft of the section on the important, and often neglected, topic of insect pests.

Astronomer Jaymie Matthews, of the University of British Columbia's Department of Physics and Astronomy, read through the celestial navigation section of Chapter four, gently correcting my errors and making a substantial contribution, including figure 4.1, to this very important topic.

Dr. Micheal Swangard, an expert in hypothermia and the developer of the hypothermia classification system used in the book, reviewed Chapter 1.

Thanks also to Dr. Judy Issac-Renton, professor of medical microbiology, who checked the chapter about water and waterborne diseases for accuracy and made many useful suggestions and recommendations.

And finally, thanks to everyone else who contributed in ways large and small to a book which has been a labor of love for me. Thanks to all those who accompanied me on various trips and to those happy souls met along the trail.

INTRODUCTION

For some, venturing into the wilderness is a choice, something different to do on a weekend, a diversion. For me there has never been a choice; it is a craving that is never satisfied. I feel at home and at peace in the bush, where I can strip away the trivial and unimportant, at least for a while, and get down to basics: staying warm and dry, finding water, getting enough to eat. While in the wilderness everyday concerns are minimal and my focus becomes much more defined.

One summer I spent a month in the remote north country traveling without radio or newspapers. When I returned to "civilization" I suddenly found listening to news broadcasts harsh and unsettling; after a month of no news I was confronted with rapes, murders, disasters and wars. I wish everyone could step outside the confines of their lives for a time.

Increasingly, people are hiking, as a means of escape, rejuvenation and reflection. Hiking to a mountaintop to drink in the scenery; stopping by a lake or stream to watch the ripples on the surface; or perhaps just sitting on a log listening to the leaves rustle in the wind.

As a young person I thrived on the physical challenge. Pick a place on a map or a point I could see in the distance: a lake or a peak. Then try to get there — trail or no trail, good weather or bad. How hard could I push myself?

For me there will always be a thrill in seeing animals in their natural habitat. Nature lovers and photographers will never run out of plants and animals to identify and photograph. Mushrooms which spring up after the rain will be gone soon. With every change in season, weather, or time of day the picture changes. A lush green tree of summer becomes yellow or red in autumn, then icy and snow laden in winter. Overcast days bring diffuse light and soft shadows. Morning mists may change into bright skies by noon and an amber glow at sunset.

Hiking is surely the most accessible and egalitarian of the outdoor pursuits. There is no licence to buy or reservations to make. The rewards are fresh air, exercise, the joy of nature and the opportunity to become better acquainted with one's friends.

There is a romance and tradition to hiking. The horse and canoe were certainly important in the exploration of North America and the expansion of the fur trade. But it is on foot that so much was accomplished and so much terrain was explored. Although canoes and horses can travel many places, a man on foot can move year round even when rivers are frozen and the snow is piled deep. In the late 1800s Dr. John Rae traveled 23,000 miles (37,000 km) on foot on various mapping expeditions to the Arctic. I have met men in Alaska who still spend the winter deep in the bush tending traplines and, eschewing dogs, pulling their own sleds. There is scarcely a place in North America, however wild, where a prospector has not walked. Explorers, trappers, and aboriginal people have stories to tell and I have included a few in this book.

A hike is more than simply a long walk. Some may consider a half hour trip through an urban park to be a hike while others would consider anything less than a half day exertion to be just a walk. Whether for a day or a month, I consider a hike to include some measure of self-reliance. This means the hiker must address the basics of survival and be prepared for the unexpected: injuries, weather changes, equipment failure and the like. Increasingly search and rescue volunteers are called upon to rescue individuals who have failed to provide for themselves. The chief reason for this failure is a lack of knowledge of the fundamentals of bush travel.

It was a concern for safety which caused a friend to ask me to speak to her son about hiking. He wanted to start hiking, but didn't know what to take, where to go and how to be safe. When we met, the two or three hours flew by and I had barely scratched the surface. What had taken a lifetime to learn could not be passed on in a few hours. What has been written about hiking generally falls into two categories. Guidebooks describe where to go, and gear books describe what to buy. This book is neither. There is certainly no shortage of guidebooks. The best known and most traveled trails are well-described in books. There are books and magazines and a legion of willing sales clerks ready to describe all manner of hiking gear. Unfortunately, the generation of trappers, prospectors, and native people who lived close to the land are for the most part, gone now and their knowledge has vanished with them. In their place are outdoor enthusiasts thirsting for the peace, challenge, and beauty that can only be satisfied by traveling in wild places. New hikers are often bursting with questions. How can we get safe water? What about bears? How do you use a compass? What about a GPS? This book is my attempt to fill the vacuum. Most hikers will appreciate a ready reference on navigation and compass use. The experienced hiker will find much new information: updated bear encounter strategies, the latest in GPSs (global positioning systems) and PLBs (personal locator beacons), a description of the psychology of being lost, a simplified approach to hypothermia, the emerging issue of waterborne diseases, lyme disease, an assessment of breathable fabrics, insect pests and much more.

This is a hands-on practical guide to hiking. The book's emphasis on safety is unmistakable. As a search and rescue volunteer, I am frequently in the bush searching for those who have more confidence than skill, some with fatal results. This book will hopefully make hiking a safer, more enjoyable experience.

1.

STAYING WARM AND DRY

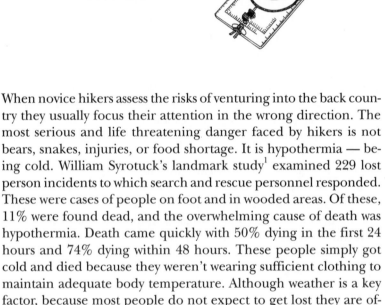

When novice hikers assess the risks of venturing into the back country they usually focus their attention in the wrong direction. The most serious and life threatening danger faced by hikers is not bears, snakes, injuries, or food shortage. It is hypothermia — being cold. William Syrotuck's landmark study[1] examined 229 lost person incidents to which search and rescue personnel responded. These were cases of people on foot and in wooded areas. Of these, 11% were found dead, and the overwhelming cause of death was hypothermia. Death came quickly with 50% dying in the first 24 hours and 74% dying within 48 hours. These people simply got cold and died because they weren't wearing sufficient clothing to maintain adequate body temperature. Although weather is a key factor, because most people do not expect to get lost they are often not at all prepared for the fickleness of Mother Nature, the early onset of darkness or a drastic change in the weather. Consider for a moment those individuals who were lost while there was precipitation of some kind: either below 45°F (7.2°C) with either snow or rain, or above 45°F with lots of rain. Given these conditions 53% of the adults either died or required hospitalization for hypothermia.

Safe hiking means carrying sufficient clothing for all weather which might reasonably be expected. The prudent hiker is prepared for the unexpected: an injury which means an unplanned night in the bush or a sudden rainstorm when none was predicted. The aforementioned study compared the rate of hypothermia fatalities between New York State and Washington State. Although the combined hypothermia death rate for the states studied was 11%, the rate for New York was only 2% while it stood at 22% for Washington State. A further 11% of the Washington State survivors were found to be alive although critically hypothermic and requiring hospitalization. Differing weather patterns help to explain the discrepancy. New York has dry, cold winters and Washington State has wet, cold winters. Washington's rainy weather makes skin and clothing damp or wet and hastens heat loss. New York has more predictable and stable weather. In Washington State, Pacific weather patterns come and go in all seasons and can quickly turn a warm sunny day into a cold wet one. Washington's Coast Mountains add a further complication. Weather in the mountains is notoriously unstable.

Lost hikers, out-of-bound skiers, and others seem to succumb easily to cold. We have all read about explorers, prospectors, and trappers who could thrive in such conditions. Conditioning seems to be the key.

In 1878 an expedition sponsored by the American Geographical Society became a test of man's ability to adapt to extreme cold. Four white men were to learn the ways of the Inuit and live and travel with them in the harsh, Arctic environment. Temperatures were recorded as low as -70°F (-57°C). The four lived without artificial heat in either tents or igloos during the whole of their stay. They ate a wild meat diet rich in animal fat. Over a period of 20 months they traveled 2,820 miles (4,538 km) above the Arctic Circle and emerged whole and healthy. Their return to civilization was difficult in at least one respect: the adaptation to indoor temperatures. Heinrich Klutschak[2], who chronicled their adventure, reported that:

> the greatest enemy was and remained that artificial producer of heat — the stove. According to our modest concepts a temperature of -7° to -10°C would be called normal while 1° to 2°C above zero was warm; and now we had to spend the entire day in temperatures of about 16°C! The constant influence of such heat, as this temperature literally represented to us, was quite unaccustomed and with the slightest carelessness it could be quite injurious.

Klutschak went on to observe, "It is not the cold which so often hampers Arctic travelers in the execution of their plans but purely and simply the circumstances that they spend the entire winter in overheated ships' cabins and are physically incapable of standing the great change when they make the switch to the raw spring climate outdoors." Slow adaptation is the key. After a week or two of sleeping out, we all begin to tolerate lower temperatures. Indeed they no longer seem low. Indoor temperatures become "too warm." The weekend hiker gone for a day or two makes no such adaptation. The hiker must set the proper standard for survival. Most hypothermia deaths occur in summer at temperatures well above freezing. Heat loss leading to hypothermia can occur in any season. In summer we may fail to recognize the dangers. Winter travelers in the backcountry are more likely to be aware of hypothermia and to take proper precautions. But all who use the outdoors for recreation in any season are subject to hypothermia: boaters, mountain bikers, hunters, as well as hikers.

The human brain and internal organs require that their temperature be maintained at 98.6°F (37°C). If the skin temperature is below 98.6°F, the body is giving off heat and the heat lost is being replaced by heat generated by the body. When heat loss increases, then heat generation must also increase. If heat is being lost faster than it is being replaced, the body is cooling and at some point the net heat loss must be stopped or death will result. "Hypo" means below normal, and "thermia" means heat; hence hypothermia simply means below normal body temperature. Hypothermia used to be called exposure, a term which masks the insidious nature of the condition. The term "exposure" conjures up the image of some lost soul being buffeted by icy winds. In fact, extreme temperatures are not required. As the body's core temperature drops, certain signs and symptoms become evident.

FEELING COLD

As the body becomes chilled, cold is felt and the organism reacts by attempting to conserve heat. The flow of heat to the extremities is reduced in order to maintain warmth in its vital core: the head and trunk. The core may therefore be at a normal temperature while the hands and feet grow cold. Warm blood must continue to reach the head to maintain brain function; it flows close to the surface and heat loss continues through the head. The body cannot conserve heat by withdrawing warm blood from the head. Only head coverings can reduce this heat loss. When the outside temperature is 40°F (4°C), half of body heat loss can be from the bare head. At 5°F (-15°C), three quarters of body heat can be lost from the head. The old expression, "If your feet are cold put on a hat," is a useful one to remember. A toque is an excellent choice to conserve heat when temperatures are near freezing. Other areas of major heat loss where the warm blood continues to flow near the body surface are the neck, armpits, and groin. A scarf is therefore an important item of winter clothing. Because these latter areas are heat conduits to the body's interior, they are key areas to protect from heat loss and where heat should be applied when rewarming.

Shivering is one of the best warning indicators that trouble lies ahead. It marks the boundary between just feeling cold and the beginning stages of hypothermia. If you or someone in your party begins to shiver, treat it with the seriousness it deserves. It is a warning signal. Unless you are very close to a warm shelter, stop and take steps to warm up before reaching first degree hypothermia. Small, easily digested snacks will help to keep you feeling warm during the day. Candies and chocolate bars or other sugar/carbohydrate foods are quickly digested and released into the blood. Keeping the body well hydrated with fluids is important in all seasons: summer and winter. Be sure to carry a water bottle at all times. In winter, streams or other water sources, which would be available during the summer, may be frozen. In cold weather, dehydration means lower fluid levels, and reduced blood circulation and is associated with both hypothermia and frostbite. Hypothermia has been classified into first, second, and third degrees of severity and was proposed by F.M. Swangard M.D. It was adopted by the International Commission of Alpine Rescue at their meeting in Poland in 1996.

FIRST DEGREE HYPOTHERMIA

First degree hypothermia occurs when net heat loss has continued to the point that the body's core temperature would be below normal in the 92°F to 98°F (33°C to 37°C) range. The body is continuing to generate heat by making the muscles shiver. In first degree hypothermia, shivering becomes intense and uncontrollable. Mental ability becomes impaired. The victim may become giggly, argumentative, or combative. He may not recognize that he has become hypothermic and may resist the efforts of others to assist him. Ability to accomplish complex tasks is diminished and the victim is likely to make mistakes in map reading and route finding. Poor judgment may lead to mistakes which can compound the seriousness of the situation. Speech may become difficult and the victim may become forgetful. Survival will depend on steps being taken by others in the group to stop and reverse the heat loss before the victim enters second degree hypothermia.

First degree hypothermia can be treated by first aid measures. Heat loss must be stopped or reduced and the victim warmed. The body's core can be warmed directly by giving the victim warm drinks. The best drink is a warm, clear fluid, preferably sweetened. This is better than coffee because the caffeine will have the effect of increasing blood flow to the extremities. This is counterproductive; you do not want to lose heat to the extremities. You want to retain it in the body's core. Alcohol will have the same effect. It may make the victim feel warm but it will cause further heat loss to the extremities.

Heat can be transferred from a warm object to the victim. A warm rock can be heated near the fire, wrapped in cloth to protect the skin and put on the victim's chest, under his jacket or other clothing. A water container or thermos can be filled with warm water. Heat packs are specialized external heat sources often carried in winter first aid kits. Once activated, heat packs can be used like the rock or thermos in places where the heat will be transferred directly to the body's core. The groin, chest, underarms and neck are all places which have a higher priority than feet and hands.

While not the preferred method for treating all three levels of hypothermia, heating the entire body is acceptable for the first level. A fire is an obvious source of external heat; built against a large rock, it will reflect heat and produce more warmth than a fire built in the open. Even better is a fire built a short distance away from the rock so that the party being warmed can sit near the rock receiving not only the heat from the fire but the heat being reflected off the rock. Rock will also absorb heat and radiate it back after the fire burns down. If two fires are built, the area between them will be very warm. When fingers and toes are warm it is a sign that heat has been conducted back to the body's vital core.

SECOND DEGREE HYPOTHERMIA

Body core temperature has now dropped to the 81°F to 91°F (27°C to 32°C) range. Shivering has actually decreased and been replaced by muscular rigidity. The victim may still be walking but his movements have become erratic and jerky. He is disoriented and irrational and eventually drifts into a stupor. He may not be able to do simple addition or tell you his birthdate. The body's core temperature has fallen close to the level where death can occur. Blood in a hypothermic person's extremities is much colder than the blood near their internal organs. If the cold blood from the extremities suddenly reaches the body core, the body core temperature will drop further even while the body surface is being warmed. In second degree hypothermia, death can result from cardiac arrest. This phenomena is called "after-drop." Care must be taken not to move the subject unnecessarily or roughly. Body movement produces a pumping action which may move cold blood from the extremities to the body core. Rapid rewarming may have a similar effect. Do not heat the victim rapidly in front of a fire. The key is slow and gradual rewarming. The other first degree hypothermia first aid measures can be followed. The seriousness of second degree hypothermia warrants skin to skin warming. Both the victim and a volunteer remove clothing and establish skin to skin contact. The volunteer embraces the hypothermic victim inside a sleeping bag. If possible, two volunteers, one on each side, sandwich the victim and use their body heat to rewarm the victim. This results in the desired slow gradual rewarming without application of excessive heat. First aid is not sufficient for second degree hypothermia. As soon as possible after warmth has been restored the victim should be taken to a medical facility for observation and treatment of any medical complications.

THIRD DEGREE HYPOTHERMIA

The body's core temperature is now below 81°F (27°C). The victim is unresponsive and unable to communicate. Unconsciousness may occur and there are few body reflexes. Although the victim may appear dead, do not make that assumption. It has been internationally agreed by medical authorities that hypothermia victims without vital signs should not be pronounced dead until they have been rewarmed to 97°F (36°C) and remain unresponsive to cardiopulmonary resuscitation or CPR. If the pulse is absent, CPR should be initiated. Care is necessary in taking the pulse as it may be present although not discernible. If no pulse is felt at the wrist, see if there is a pulse at the carotid artery located at the side of the neck. There are many documented cases of apparently dead people, frequently children, who have regained consciousness and made a full recovery. The emphasis now switches from rewarming to stabilizing the victim's body temperature and removal to a medical facility. This is a medical emergency. Consider helicopter evacuation to the nearest hospital. If medical help is within one or two hours, evacuation to a medical facility is best. In a hospital, rewarming can occur in a controlled manner while vital signs are being monitored. The victim should be handled with particular care to avoid the risk of after-drop. Avoid rough handling and if the victim is unconscious, maintain him in a horizontal position so as not to interrupt the existing flow of blood to the brain. If no medical help is available and evacuation to a hospital is not practical, follow the same first aid steps as for second degree hypothermia.

HYPOTHERMIA FACTORS

Temperature

Hypothermia is the end result of the body's heat loss exceeding heat generation. A hiker who gets wet in wintertime may have less than an hour to live. A summer hiker caught out overnight in T-shirt and shorts will have longer. The temperature affects the rate of heat loss. A hiker should therefore carry sufficient clothing for the worst weather possible and the lowest temperatures which may be encountered. Since there is always the chance of an unplanned night in the woods, this means clothing sufficient for nighttime as well as daytime temperatures. A thermal blanket reflects body heat back to the person and is a good addition to the first aid kit but not a substitute for extra clothing.

Wind

The wind and resulting windchill can turn a cool day into a cold one. A hiker caught on a windy mountain ridge, even on a summer day, can experience rapid heat loss. This is another good reason to carry rain gear. Rain gear offers great protection from heat robbing wind. If shivering starts, it is necessary to get out of the wind and regain body warmth. Set up a tent, get behind some rocks or behind a tree — whatever it takes to reduce the windchill.

Rain

You may trust the weather forecast, but would you bet your life on it? Dry clothing traps a warm layer of insulating air, while wet clothing holds a layer of water against the skin and as water is an excellent conductor of heat away from the body a person in wet clothing will experience rapid heat loss even on a mild summer day. Carry rain gear regardless of the weather forecast, including waterproof pants, jacket, and hat. If clothing becomes wet, heat loss will continue until it is removed. A few dry clothes are better than a lot of wet ones. And wet clothes includes underwear which is usually made of cotton, a material which retains water. Wet underwear will make your dry clothes wet, too. Take off all wet clothes. If your clothes are damp, you will be warmer in your sleeping bag without them. Extra dry clothing carried in the pack can be a lifesaver. Packs are not waterproof so be sure extra clothing is protected in a plastic or other waterproof bag.

On overnight trips, many canoeists carry a tarpaulin and cord, as well as a tent. When waiting out wet weather a small hiker's tent quickly becomes a prison. Few hikers would wish to carry both a tent and a tarpaulin but a tarp alone can make waiting out bad weather bearable. A small tarp or even a sheet of plastic can be a refuge and a place to cook, eat, lounge about, sort camping gear and do all the many chores that go with camping. Trees are never in the most convenient places for pitching the tarp, so err on the side of caution and take extra cord. It weighs very little and has lots of other uses: clothes lines, bear proofing a food cache in trees, and emergency repairs.

Tarps can be used as a makeshift tent. Indeed two hundred years ago when the courier de bois traveled across North America, they took no tents. They tucked one side of their canvas under their overturned canoes and weighted the other end of the tarp with rocks. Tarp tents lack the refinements of real tents — no bug protection, no floor, and not very wind resistant. They will however keep most of the rain and all of the dew off you and your gear. Do not make the mistake of draping the tarp directly over you like a top blanket. Moisture from your body and from the ground will condense on the underside of the tarp and you will be damp by morning. Better than nothing if it is raining, but not ideal.

A bivy sac is a bag to put your sleeping bag in. It is waterproof and zips up offering bug protection and more warmth. It is lighter than a tent and OK in a pinch but look out for condensation inside the bivy sac.

Perspiration

Rain is wetness from the outside while exertion causes dampness from the inside. The jogger pounding down the sidewalk sweats profusely. His clothing is wet and damp with sweat. He cools down, has a shower, and changes into dry clothes. The hiker may exert himself almost as much but can't afford to ignore the wet clothing. When fatigue sets in, the hiker stops and quickly feels the chill of wet clothing. Once the clothes are wet the hiker must find a way to get dry or keep moving. Far better to avoid getting damp. Layered clothing permits the hiker to keep adjusting the amount of clothing. Sufficient clothing at the start of the hike becomes too much clothing fifteen or twenty minutes later. That is the time to stop and reduce clothing before moisture builds up. I sweat easily and profusely and usually hike with a single thin layer of long sleeved polypropylene underwear on my upper body. If the polypropylene becomes wet, it dries quickly. If temperatures are low or the wind is blowing, this is not practical and I carry extra dry clothing in my pack just in case I get damp or wet. At rest stops, extra dry layers can be added and then removed when it is time to go again. When it is severely cold, adjust your pace. If you have reduced clothing and you are still hot, slow down. Gore-Tex and other breathable rain gear fabrics have a limited ability to vent moist air away from the body; they cannot be expected to vent the body completely when sweating heavily. Gore-Tex will not transport sweat or moisture after it has condensed against the fabric; it transports vapours not liquids. Higher priced jackets have "pit zips" which are underarm vents. They can be opened or closed according to need. Jacket pockets can also act like little vents — unzip them to let cooler air in and moist air out. Coated nylon or rubberized rainwear is the best possible rain protection but also blocks moist air escaping from the body. Open up the jacket and pump out warm, moist air before it turns to sweat.

Wet Brush

Brush becomes wet as a result of rain, but it also holds dew. In the autumn when nighttime temperatures fall, the brush can be loaded with as much water as if it had rained. Fall days mean the sun is lower in the sky. More areas are shaded, the sun takes longer to climb in the sky and simply cannot dry the brush as well as in the summer. The brush can stay wet all day. Push through the under-brush and legs and pants become soaked. Soon the dew will be running down your legs into your socks and your feet are wet. If the brush is shoulder high, your jacket will be soaked too. If it is over your head, touching a small conifer can bring a cold shower or most unpleasantly, a soft snowball on your head or down your neck.

Rain Gear

Waterproof rain pants and jacket are a must. To keep feet dry, put the tops of gaiters under the rain pants. This means the water will roll down the pants and on top of the gaiters. If the gaiters are over the pants, the water goes under the gaiters and into the boots. When walking in snow, the gaiters go over the pants so snow does not get pushed under the pant leg. Pushing through wet underbrush, branches rub against the clothing depositing water and rubbing it in. Surface preparations applied to breathable wa-terproof type clothing wash off and the outside becomes wet. Moisture cannot be transported through the wet surface. When this happens the breathable fabric is no longer breathable. It has "wet out." Sometimes breathable fabrics break down entirely. Several years ago on a week-long hike near the Yukon/British Columbia border, it rained every day and night and when it wasn't raining, the brush was loaded with water. For the most part we followed animal trails — pushing through heavy brush most of the time. After breakfast, I would strip off my dry clothing and put on wet rain gear. Even when I dried the rainwear the night before, it soon got soaked by the brush. All day I would stay wet pushing through the underbrush. I would keep warm by hiking without stopping for long. In the evening if it was not raining, I would take off my wet clothes and put on dry clothes to wear around camp. In the morning it would be off with the dry clothes and on with the wet again. This story illustrates several points; rain gear can break down as well as wet out (see Chapter 14 for more information on rainwear). Always carry extra clothing so that you have something dry to change into if you become wet. Do not get all your clothing wet, even if this means wearing damp clothing and saving the dry. In my case the nights were cold and I needed dry clothing to wear inside my sleeping bag. I was comfortable enough during the day as long as I kept moving and my body was generating heat. Don't wear wet or damp clothing inside your sleeping bag. If your sleeping bag is going to keep you warm, it must be kept dry.

If you travel long enough in wet conditions, your feet will be wet. It is impossible to dry boots in a tent or by a fire. Leather dries slowly. I carry a second pair of socks but find that if I put dry socks in wet boots I end up with two pairs of wet socks. If your camp shoes are still dry or you like to wear socks to bed — keep the second pair dry and keep the wet pair for hiking.

Conduction

Conduction is the transfer of heat away from the body into the ground, air, water or snow. Everyone likes to rest sitting down — the question is what do you sit on? One solution is to load the pack so that all clothing and the sleeping bag is at the bottom of the pack. Anything breakable or bendable can go in a side pocket or towards the top. Sit on the bottom portion of the pack. In this way you can sit on a warm seat regardless of weather. You will retain body heat and feel more comfortable. On day hikes when the extra bulk doesn't matter, I often carry a piece of old foam sleeping pad. It feels warm even when sitting on snow.

Sleeping pads are not just for comfort. When sleeping out, heat is lost both into the air and into the ground. One can sleep quite comfortably on snow provided one has a good barrier to prevent heat loss by conduction. Do not underestimate the amount of heat lost by conduction — piling more layers on top will not keep you warm unless you also add layers underneath.

Typically, hikers carry three-quarter size sleeping pads which do not extend to the lower legs. Put a layer of rain gear or other clothing under the lower legs to keep an insulating layer between you and the ground to prevent heat loss. Spruce boughs are the traditional insulator which was used before sleeping pads. Now it is not necessary to use trees unless one is injured and the "no trace philosophy" (which dictates that we should leave the wilderness as we find it, leaving nothing but footprints and taking nothing but pictures) goes out the window. Break the soft ends off the boughs and create a soft, insulating layer. There are different species of spruce but any will do. The general characteristic of this evergreen is a conical shape and near horizontal branches. The branches have needles on all sides and it is this characteristic which makes them soft to lie on.

Fig. 1.1: Characteristic spruce tree profile; tip of spruce bough.

Physical Factors

There are clearly physical factors at work in our ability to withstand the elements. After sleeping out in cold weather for a while,
I have trouble sleeping at normal room temperatures. Tradition-
ally, native people and the first Europeans were accustomed to an
ambient temperature far below what we would consider normal.
They survived in conditions which would kill most modern
urbanites. Children are less able to tolerate low temperatures as
they have more skin surface to radiate heat in proportion to body
mass and their high metabolic rate crashes at night requiring extra bedding. The elderly have a reduced ability to vasoconstrict,
meaning that when exposed to cold they are less able to reduce
the flow of warm blood to their hands and feet. They will lose heat
at a greater rate than a younger person. For them gloves, scarves,
and warm footwear are very important. In addition, the elderly,
with reduced muscle tone, will be less able to generate body heat
through shivering. Alcohol and caffeine both affect the body and
counteract the body's attempts to conserve heat by vasoconstric-
tion. Candy and carbohydrates keep the blood sugar level up and
the body's furnace fuelled. Diabetics with their difficulty in maintaining constant blood sugar are therefore at increased risk.

BAD WEATHER TIPS

Much of my hiking is done on the west coast of British Columbia,
sometimes called the "wet coast," with rain, high humidity, clouds,
and limited sunshine. Lower elevations are more likely given over

to urbanization and forestry. The wilderness areas tend to be those areas left — steeper, higher elevations with more rock and snow. These can be dripping with moisture while lower elevations enjoy sunshine. Hiking in wet conditions requires extra care. Once you or your gear gets wet you will likely stay wet or get wetter. Fire making is difficult. The longer you stay out in the wet, the more clothing and gear will become wet. Do everything possible to stay dry as long as possible.

Packs are more water-resistant than waterproof. Zippers, stitching and hard wear conspire to make the gear inside your pack wet. External frame packs are no longer in fashion but do have the advantage of having waterproof covers available. These covers slip over the top of the pack and are pulled down over the back before being tucked under. A drawstring tightens the cover although the shoulder straps keep the cover from completely enveloping the pack. Internal frame backpacks cannot be kept entirely dry, so it is the contents of the pack which must be waterproofed. With the pack itself providing abrasion protection, a plastic garbage bag can be put inside the bag as a liner. (An orange plastic garbage bag is better than a dark one. If one is lost, an orange bag is a good emergency signaling device and is highly visible to searchers against the green background of the bush.) If a large expedition pack is being used rather than a day-pack, multiple garbage bags should be used to subdivide the pack's contents. Certainly the sleeping bag should have its own garbage bag. Opening a large pack to look for something usually means stacking the contents on the ground while searching for the desired item. This exposes the contents of the pack to moisture from the ground as well as rain from above. Far better to break the contents down into separate waterproof bags. Use whatever system makes sense, then stick to it. Sleeping bag in its own stuff sack plus garbage bag; emergency clothing next in its own waterproof bag; heavy clothing also separate; on top of that goes hats, gloves and the clothing being taken off and put on throughout the day. Rain gear can go in its own bag — this time to keep the moisture inside and away from dry clothing. It helps to have different coloured bags so you can quickly find which bag you are after without having to pull all the bags out of the pack and expose them to rain. Gaiters can go in a side pocket where they can't get anything wet. Thick plastic food bags are a good idea for individual items: camera, food, socks, maps, etc. The free produce bags given away at the supermarket are too fragile.

Buy good quality plastic bags.

A great deal of care should be taken with the sleeping bag. Nights are always colder than days; reduced activity means less body heat is being produced. Bodily injury or bad weather will mean a great deal of time spent in your sleeping bag. Rain, wet brush or submersion in a stream during a fording can all spell disaster for your sleeping bag. Waterproof packaging is a must. Down bags are lighter and compact better but I prefer synthetic bags. Moisture will cause a down bag to loose its heat-insulating ability much more than a synthetic bag. Warm bodies in a tent on a cool night mean lots of condensation inside the tent. It is paradoxical that when the weather gets cool the need for ventilation increases. Cool air can carry less moisture than warm air. Keep the tent well ventilated in order to keep your sleeping bag and clothing dry. Clothing won't dry out in a small backpacking tent, it's too moist inside. Keep clothes in a waterproof bag when inside the tent. This will stop moist air getting to them and will stop them getting wet should they touch the inner wall of the tent. When inside the sleeping bag, do not breathe into the bag. The moisture from your breath will make it damp. If the sleeping bag isn't enough to keep you warm put on extra clothes. I keep extra clothes at hand so that during the night I can add clothes as the temperature drops. Beginning in the fall, a toque can keep you warm inside the sleeping bag because it prevents heat loss from the important head region. If using a mummy-type sleeping bag remember to pull the drawstrings to close up the bag while leaving a clear opening for nose and mouth. Every time you change positions in the bag, the movement of your body will pump warm air out and cool air in. Draw the drawstrings. Two people zipped together in regular sleeping bags will have a space between them where cold air can enter. All right in the summer but definitely cold when the temperature drops.

If the sleeping bag is moist in the morning, try to dry it out while doing camp chores. If it's dry outside, spread it on some branches. Make taking down the tent the last camp chore so that it gets as much chance to dry out as possible. A wet tent is heavier than a dry one. When making camp set up the tent and spread out the sleeping bag as soon as you stop. This will give both sleeping bag and tent a further chance to dry out before bedtime. At night an extra garbage bag is almost essential if your pack is to be left outside. Use it to place over the top of your pack. It will protect it from rain and dew.

Matches must always be kept dry. Curl two packages of matches into an empty film canister. I've not found that waterproof store bought matches work very well. I know that traditional bush travelers dipped wooden match heads in paraffin. I suspect they were lacking a truly waterproof container. Ordinary matches work well as long as you keep them dry.

---

1   Syrotuck, *Analysis of Lost Person Behavior*

2   Klutshak, *Overland to Starvation Cove, with the Inuit in Search of Franklin 1878 – 1880*

2.

MAPS

WHERE TO GET THEM

The most basic source of information for hikers and the most universally available is the topographic map. Topographic maps, or "topos," are available to the public at reasonable cost for every part of the United States and Canada. The mapping system used in both countries is similar but not identical. Both countries make maps available through a series of local distributors in each country. For further information contact:

In the US: Distribution Branch
     U.S. Geological Survey
     Box 25286
     Denver Federal Center
     Denver, Colorado
     80225

In Canada: Canada Map Office
     Products and Services Division
     Dept. of Energy, Mines and Resources
     Ottawa, Ontario
     K1A 0E9

Maps are identified by a map name and number and it is necessary to obtain an index for your area of interest so that you can identify and order the correct map. In the United States an index and catalog is available for each state. Simply order the index and catalog for the appropriate area. In Canada there are three indexes and you will need to specify which index you require: Western Canada, Eastern Canada, or Canada's far north. If you do not know which index to order state the latitude and longitude of the area you are interested in.

MAP SCALE

The next step will be to decide what map scale is most appropriate for your needs. Large scale maps cover less ground area but the geographic features are large and easy to see. Large scale maps provide the most detail. Small scale maps cover more ground area. If interested in a number of places in the same area you may be able to save money by buying a single small scale map. A scale of 1:50,000 means that a given distance on the ground is 50,000 times greater than as measured on the map. Therefore 1 cm on the map is 50,000 cm (or 0.5 km) on the ground.

Common map scales are:

1:250,000	1 centimeter = 2.5 kilometers
	1 inch = approx. 4 miles
1:125,000	1 centimeter = 1.25 kilometers
	1 inch = approx. 2 miles
1:100,000	1 centimeter = 1 kilometer
	1 inch = approx. 1.6 miles
1: 62,500	1 inch = approx. 1 mile
	1 centimeter = 0.6 kilometer
1: 50,000	1 centimeter = 0.5 kilometer
	1 inch = approx. 0.8 miles

For a short hike in rugged terrain on a poorly-marked trail use 1:50,000. If the country is less rugged, the trail is good, or a large number of maps would be needed, a smaller scale map will do. A 1:125,000 may be satisfactory. One disadvantage of large scale detailed maps is that there will be fewer geographical features to establish positions from. A mountain is an excellent reference point to use to establish position, but if it is off the map, it will be lost as a possible reference point. You may wish to order and carry topographic maps of different scale, a large scale topographic map for terrain detail and a small scale topographic map for distant landmarks.

MEASURING DISTANCES

Topographic maps have lines drawn on them which divide the map into squares or grids. These grid lines make estimating distances easy. On a metric 1:50,000 scale topographic map, the grid lines are 2 cm or 1 km apart. If your trail goes 5 grid lines east, then it is going 5 km east. On a 1:250,000 map the grid lines are 4 km square. Five grid lines equals 20 km. Remember that this is a theoretical distance — it assumes that the land is flat and ignores changes in elevation. It is also "as the crow flies." Hikers follow winding trails or topographic features while the map tends to ignore the smaller twists and turns. In either case "trail miles are longer than "map miles."

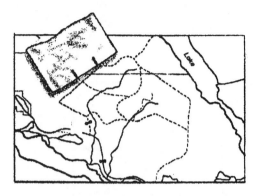

Fig. 2.1: Measuring marks made on the edge of a piece of paper.

Every topographic map will have a ruler depicted on the border to help convert map distances to ground distances. The Silva Ranger compass has a ruler in both centimeters and inches along its base plate. Measure

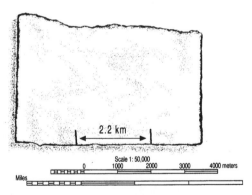

Fig. 2.2: Measuring with map ruler.

the map distance with the compass ruler, then either calculate the ground distance or hold the compass along the map ruler to read off the ground distance. If it is longer than the compass ruler a different technique can be used. Use a piece of paper or turn down the edge of the map to mark off the distance to be measured. The markings can then be held along the map ruler to determine ground distance.

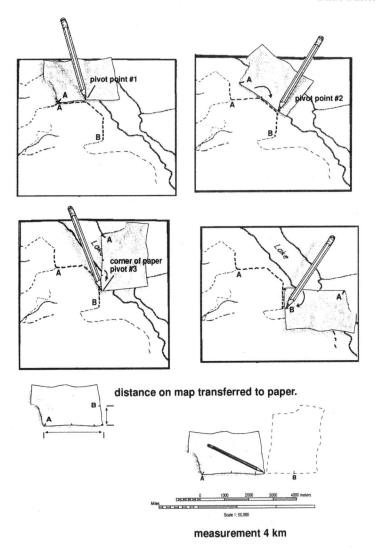

distance on map transferred to paper.

measurement 4 km

Fig. 2.3: Using pivot points to measure around bends.

There are times when "as the crow" distances are not good enough. Here are three options:

1. Instead of measuring the distance on the map as a single straight line, consider the route as a series of smaller straight lines. Hold the edge of a piece of paper along the first section of the trail with the corner of the paper at the trailhead. Mark the corner of

the paper which is next to the trailhead. Press the edge of the paper with a pen point near the point where the trail makes its first turn. Pivot the paper around the pen point to bring the edge of the piece of paper parallel with the new direction of the trail. Press again with the pen point where the trail makes its next turn. Pivot the paper so that it follows each new trail direction. Note that you can continue around the corner of the page by pivoting at the corner and continuing along the next side. When you get to the end of the trail, make a measuring mark on your page. Hold the page along the map ruler and read off the length of the trail.

2. This technique requires a string, shoelace or perhaps the cord of your compass. Hold one end of the string at the position of the trailhead on your map. Shape the string along the trail route shown on the map. Be sure the string is not stretchy. Hold it along the map ruler and measure off the trail length.

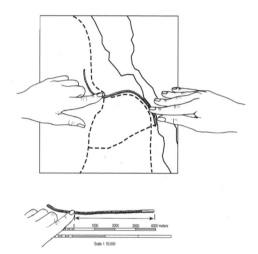

Fig. 2.4: Measuring with a string.

3. If greater accuracy is important to you, use a map measurer. These are relatively inexpensive instruments which are light and small enough to go in your pack. A small wheel on the bottom of the device is rolled along the route shown on your map. The small

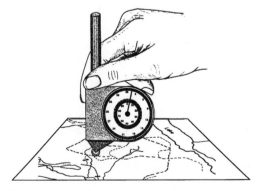

Fig. 2.5: Accurate measurement using a map measurer.

wheel turns a larger wheel and the distance traveled is shown on the larger wheel. If the scale of the map is different from any on the map measurer, then use the map measurer to measure the map distance in inches or centimeters. You can then run the map measurer back along the map ruler to calculate the distance.

CONTOUR LINES

The distinguishing characteristic of a topographic map is its contour lines. The contour lines identify all points of the same elevation. To travel directly up or down a slope, one would travel at 90° to the contour lines.

The topographic map is a two dimensional piece of paper but the contour lines allow it to represent the surface of the earth

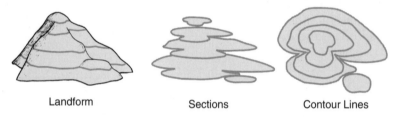

Landform   Sections   Contour Lines

Fig. 2.6: Contour lines identify all points on the ground which have the same elevation. The view is from above.

which has three dimensions. With a little practice, you will easily be able to tell the ridges from valleys and the good routes from the bad.

A topographic map will state the contour interval on the margin. A contour interval of 100 ft (30.5 m) means that each contour line is 100 feet higher or lower than the one beside it. If a hike takes you up ten contour lines, then you will be climbing 1,000 ft (305 m) in addition to the horizontal distance which you have measured on the map. Some contour lines are thicker than others, usually every fifth one. In our example the thick lines would be 500 (5 x 100) feet apart. Because they are thick they are more easily identified and traced with a finger across the map. If you have many contour lines to cross, the thick lines can be counted and multiplied by five.

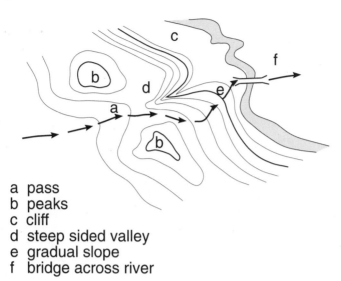

a pass
b peaks
c cliff
d steep sided valley
e gradual slope
f bridge across river

Fig. 2.7: Contour lines are used for route finding. Note: The mountain peaks at "b" and the bridge at "f" are visible reference points which can be sighted through a compass to establish one's position.

We have already discussed techniques for measuring horizontal distances between points on the map. This technique ignores the extra distance traveled to gain or lose elevation. Remember the Pythagorean theorem from high school geometry? The square of the distance traveled along the hypotenuse is the square of the horizontal distance plus the square of the vertical distance. An easier way to approximate the total distance is to add 1/3 of the vertical elevation change to the horizontal distance.

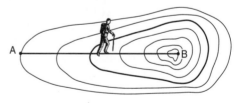

Fig. 2.8: 10 cm of map distance equals 5 km of horizontal distance when using a 1:50,000 scale map; 7 contour lines at 40 m contour intervals equals 280 m of additional vertical distance.

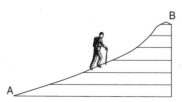

Remember that the shorter the contour interval the more accurate the map. Do not make any assumptions about the ground between the contour lines. The topographic map simply does not provide this information. Consider the following:

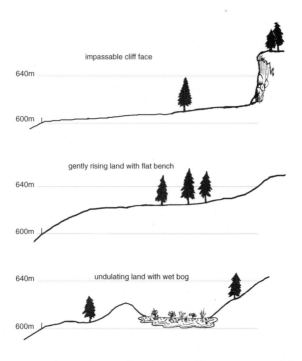

Fig. 2.9: Do not make conclusions about the ground between contour lines. These different landforms will have identical contour lines.

MAP LIMITATIONS

While the contour lines can be considered accurate, be aware that the map may contain other information which is not. Check the margin of the map for the copyright or publication date. Do you have the most recent edition? Check also the year in which the information was collected to produce the map. I can recall hiking out of the bush to a logging road which lay on the opposite side of a river. A bridge was clearly marked on the map with an old access road to the bridge. Unfortunately, the river had washed out the bridge and a good section of the road several years after the map was made. Reliance on the map meant a half day lost hiking to a bridge that no longer existed. Man-made features become less reliable the older the map is. In steep terrain, roads which are not maintained quickly wash out and can become impassable.

Old logging roads may be clearly marked on the map but be barely recognizable on the ground. Fast-growing species of trees reestablish themselves and begin to grow in the roadbed. The species of tree which first establishes itself is a lighter green than the older trees of the forest. Frequently the course of an old logging road can be seen from a distance by following the light green foliage snaking through the more mature and darker forest. The light green color will also identify watercourses and scree slopes where erosion and water movement has killed large mature trees and young trees have established themselves. Old cabins may show on the map but be nothing more than a pile of rubble on the ground. Much of the information for topographic maps is taken from the air. Many trails and roads are missed and will not appear on the map and any built since the date of your map will certainly not be on it. Seasonal variation means that streams and bogs may appear or disappear according to whether the information was collected in a dry or wet spell. Be particularly careful of heavy rains. The small streams shown on your map can become raging torrents if they drain a large enough area. Even if following a good trail it may become impassable due to flooding if you get there after heavy rain.

GRID NORTH, TRUE NORTH, AND MAGNETIC NORTH

Most map users know that north is at the top and south is at the bottom. The hiker needs much more detailed and precise information and that information is all contained on the topographic map. Failure to read and understand the declination information provided on the map means that the compass will not be set properly and accurate route finding will not be possible.

Topographic maps are gridded (have squares drawn over them) as previously discussed. Therefore they contain three different norths:

grid north:	This is the direction of the vertical grid lines (more accurately: the direction of the grid line in the middle of the map).
true north:	This is the direction of the geographic

north pole and the direction we are interested in for route finding. It must be calculated.

magnetic north: This is the direction of the magnetic north pole. It is the place the red needle of the compass points to.

CALCULATING MAGNETIC DECLINATION

The compass points to magnetic north but we need to know the direction of true north. The angle between magnetic north and true north is called the declination and once this angle has been calculated, you will be able to add or subtract it from the direction that the compass needle points. In southern Canada and in the US (outside Alaska) the declination for maps in the same area will be almost the same so that the declination need not be changed unless traveling hundreds of miles. In Alaska and northern Canada, declination can vary one to two degrees between places on the same 1:250,000 map and more detailed information is provided on these topographic maps.

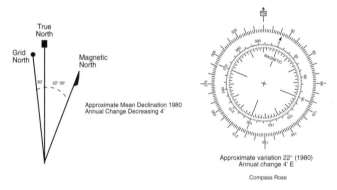

Fig. 2.10: Two different ways to represent magnetic declination information on topograhic maps.

22° This is the difference between magnetic north and true north in 1980. True north is 22° west of magnetic north.

30' This is the error inherent in the map maker's attempt to portray the three dimensional surface of the earth on a two dimensional piece of paper. It is the angle between grid north and true north. If you don't use grid lines or you don't want to fuss over .5°, just ignore it.

60'   In 1980 the difference between true north and magnetic north was 22°. The following year and for each subsequent year the 22° was reduced by 4'. By 1995, 15 years had passed and the declination was reduced by a total of 60'(15 x 4').

If using the grid lines and trying to be as accurate as possible, the declination angle between the grid lines and magnetic north must be known. The calculation is as follows:

1980 angle between true north and magnetic north   22°00'

Add: angle between grid north and true north   30'

Subtract: decrease in declination between 1980 and
    1995 (60' or 1°)   1°00'

Equals: declination from grid north to magnetic north   21°30'

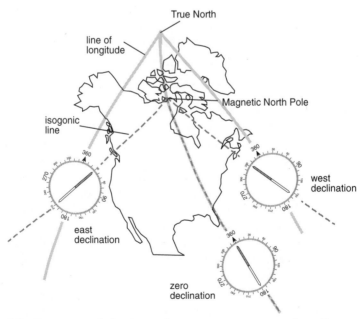

Fig. 2.11: The magnetic declination can be east, west, or even zero, depending on one's location.

If not using grids, we would not add 30' and the declination would be 21° west. As a practical matter 30' is within the margin of accuracy of a hand-held compass and such a minor variation is almost irrelevant. The direction of grid north seldom differs from true north by more than 2°. Use anything close to 21°30' or 21°.

Generally, inexpensive compasses do not have a declination adjustment and are therefore not appropriate for hikers. Follow the manufacturer's instructions for setting the declination. Usually a small screwdriver is needed. The Silva Ranger compass comes with a small metal screwdriver for this purpose.

At sea, calculating the declination of a marine compass can be a matter of some complexity since the ship contains metal and electrical currents. Some hikers follow the mariners' practice of not using declination. By setting the compass declination at zero, the compass will point to magnetic north but the map will still have true north at the top. The map must then be reoriented to magnetic rather than true north by drawing parallel lines across the maps along the magnetic north/south axis. If this sounds confusing, don't attempt it. I don't intend to try it either. To me north means true north and that is always at the top of the map. Take a few moments to do the declination adjustment calculation, adjust your compass, then forget about it. As long as you are hiking in the same general area, you need not reset your compass. In our example, you can knock off a degree every 15 years.

GRID LINES AND GRID COORDINATES

The grid lines on the map divide a topographic map in a way similar to a street map. One can refer to a location by using horizontal and vertical grid coordinates. Hikers find this system easier than using latitude and longitude coordinates. The grid coordinate numbers increase from west to east (left to right) and south to north (bottom to top). The grid line on the horizontal is always read first. Thus a grid coordinate of 170 720 would be grid number 17 on the horizontal and 72 on the vertical. The third digit gives us a more exact position. If we are given a position of 175 721, then on the horizontal axis our position would be midway between 17 and 18. On the vertical axis our position would be 0.1 of the distance from 72 to 73. The truly determined can try for a fourth digit. The use of grid coordinates allows communication of a position without pointing to the place on the map. You can communicate the position over the telephone or write it in your notes. Having the grid coordinates will help to find the position later on the map and avoids having to mark the map.

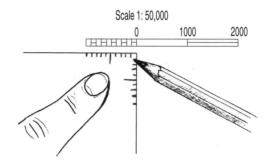

Fig. 2.12: Making a romer on the corner of a piece of scrap paper.

To make reading positions easier a "romer"(also spelled roamer) is used. A Silva Ranger compass has a romer on it for 1:50,000 maps, you can buy a romer and keep it in your wallet, or best of all make one. Take the corner of a page and hold it against the map to measure back from the corner of the page exactly one grid space. Mark the other side of the corner one grid space back from the corner. Hold the corner of the page against the ruler scale at the bottom of the map. Subdivide each grid space distance into tenths. You now have a romer.

Now hold the romer against the map with the corner of the romer at the place you are interested in. Read the grid coordinates. Your position is 175-721.

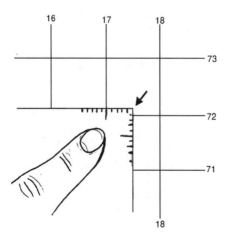

Fig. 2.13: Using a romer to find grid coordinates 175-721.

LATITUDE AND LONGITUDE

Although most hikers will find grid coordinates easier to use than latitude and longitude, pilots and mariners use latitude and longitude so an understanding of the terminology can be important when talking to pilots or reading charts.

Lines of latitude are the horizontal lines running parallel to the equator and numbering zero at the equator to 90° at the north and south pole. Lines of longitude run north south between the north and south pole. Lines of west longitude run from zero at Greenwich, England, to 180° at a location west of Hawaii.

Horizontal grid line numbers and latitude degrees are shown on each side of a topographic map. Both sets of numbers increase from south to north. Vertical grid line numbers and longitude degrees are shown on the top and bottom of the map. Vertical grid line numbers increase from west to east while longitude degrees increase from east to west. This sometimes causes confusion. Be sure to read the correct set of numbers and interpolate the longitudes correctly so that you add longitude minutes when you go left. Also note that grid lines are not perfectly parallel to lines of latitude and longitude. The lines of longitude converge at the north pole and are not parallel to each other. This means a degree of latitude is not a fixed distance. It gets smaller the further north one goes. A degree of latitude is usually a shorter distance than a degree of longitude. Check the scales carefully along the edges of the map. When citing the latitude and longitude of a position, the latitude is given first followed by the longitude. Measure along the sides of the map first to get the latitude. On a 1:50,000 map, the numbers represent minutes (60 seconds equals 1 minute). If looking for latitude 49°17'20" (49 degrees, 17 minutes, 20 seconds), you should first check to see that you have the right map. Does your map have 49°15' to 49°20' on it? If there are no second markings, you will have to estimate where 20 seconds would be. Find 49°17' along the edge then go up 1/3 (20/60) of the way to 49°18' and mark the spot on the edge. The same procedure applies to the lines of longitude except that you will be reading along either the top or bottom of the map. Remember to measure from right to left. Then mark the spot. Your position is where the lines of latitude and longitude intersect. You can cheat and use the nearest grid lines to approximate the position on the map or be more precise and use a yardstick and pencil to obtain the exact position.

It is difficult to find the seconds if none are shown on the map. We tend to think in terms of decimals rather than 60ths. A trick is to round the seconds to the nearest 5 seconds to get the closest 12th. Thus 4 seconds is 5/60ths or 1/12th; 11 seconds is 10/60ths or 1/6th; and 17 seconds is 15/60ths or 1/4.

MAP CARE AND MAP FOLDING

Paper maps can self-destruct very quickly. Plastic maps are available for certain popular national, state, and provincial parks. Many are published by Trails Illustrated, PO Box 3610, Evergreen, Colorado, 80439. These maps are waterproof and generally more durable than paper maps. Liquid products are available which are applied to maps to make the paper waterproof. These are not widely used. Clear self-adhesive shelving plastic works well on small maps. The map is sandwiched between the sheets of plastic. With proper care a paper map should last a long time even without these products.

Most topographic maps come unfolded and rolled. Be very careful with the placement of the folds in a map. They will become the tear lines where the map will eventually rip. I keep my maps in resealable freezer bags. Some of these bags come with an opaque panel for writing on the bag. Avoid these. Plastic map cases are also available which enable one to read the map while it is inside the case. You can stand in the rain with a stiff wind blowing and the map will be dry and protected. The only time a map needs to be taken out of its case is to turn to a different portion of the map. If the area of interest crosses two maps, carry both maps in separate cases or cut out the areas required and glue them on a single page of paper. In order to minimize handling, it is recommended that the map face outward

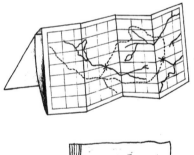

Fig. 2.14: Map folded "map side" out to fit in a map cover.

and the folds be planned so that the map fits the map case.

I usually spread my map out on the floor and use a yardstick to plan the folds. Once you have one map folded, use it as a template to mark the folds for later maps. Take care of your map and it will take care of you. It may be tempting to save money by having one map for the entire group of hikers but this means one person has all the information and the rest of the group are followers. If the parties become separated someone will have no map. If you find other maps which contain useful or more up-to-date information take them along, too. Watch for extra information about trails or roads, and take the trouble before you leave home to mark this information on your topographic map (in pencil of course). Marking maps precisely is an exacting task better done at the kitchen table than sitting on a log with the map on your knee. I take a pencil to make notes or marks on the map. You can keep your notes or a journal on the back of the map thus consolidating many separate pieces of information. After the hike you will always know where your notes are.

3.

THE COMPASS

In the previous chapter on maps we calculated magnetic declination using the information provided on a topographic map. The magnetic declination is the angle between where the compass needle points (magnetic north) and true north (or grid north).

When a compass is purchased, the declination will be set to zero. There are places in North America where magnetic north will be the same as true north, but the odds of being in such a place are remote. True north will normally be either east or west of magnetic north. This means that there are two steps to be taken before you will be able to use a compass. First the angle of magnetic declination must be calculated (see Chapter 2). Next, the compass must be adjusted by this amount to compensate for the declination. Cheap compasses may not have a declination adjustment and are not suitable for route finding. It is theoretically possible to calculate the declination then add or subtract it from your bearing every time you use the compass. Under actual trail conditions this is impractical and errors are inevitable. Save money somewhere else. In wilderness areas, your life often depends on your compass. I have used the same compass for over thirty years and it works as well now as the day I bought it. Newer compasses may have a few extra features but are no better for basic route finding. A top of the line compass is cheap if used for a few decades.

Remember that the earth's magnetic lines of force will bend around metal objects. A hand-held compass will not work in a car. You risk compass error if you hold a compass near steel rimmed glasses, a steel belt buckle, or if you hold a knife or other metal object while using it. There are special situations where large underground ore bodies cause compass error. There have been times over the years when I have been disoriented to the point of wondering if my compass could be in error. Each time this has happened, I've stopped to think things over and found that I had made some kind of error. Trust your compass. The Silva Ranger compass has been adopted in British Columbia for search and rescue operations.

PARTS OF A COMPASS

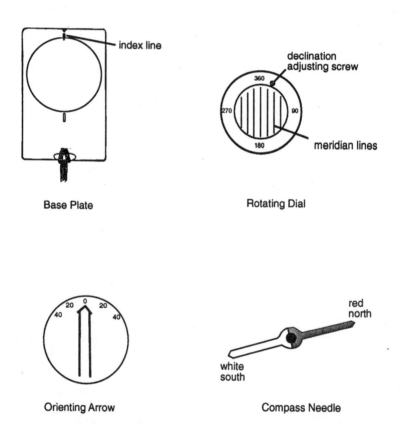

Fig. 3.1: The four parts of a basic compass.

1. COMPASS NEEDLE – The compass needle is balanced on a pivot so that it is free to turn in any direction no matter where the rest of the compass is pointed. As long as the compass is held level, the red end of the compass needle will always point to magnetic north.

2. ORIENTING ARROW – The orienting arrow is attached to the rotating dial. When the rotating dial is turned, the orienting arrow turns with it. When the compass is being used and the compass is held level the compass needle will swing into alignment. The red end of the needle will point to magnetic north. The rotating dial is then turned by hand and the orienting arrow turns too. Turn the orienting arrow to point in the same direction as the compass needle. Both the orienting needle and the compass needle will then be pointing to magnetic north.

3. ROTATING DIAL – Turning the declination adjusting screw will turn the orienting arrow but not the rotating dial. If the magnetic declination is to be set at 22° east of true north, then the declination adjusting screw is turned so that the orienting arrow will point to 22° east of north on the rotating dial's declination scale. Once this adjustment has been made, the orienting arrow will be fixed in its new position. The 22° east differential between the rotating dial and the orienting arrow will be maintained whenever the rotating dial is turned.

4. BASE PLATE – The base plate holds the rotating dial and orienting arrow in position but allows them to turn. The orienting arrow is attached to the rotating dial and can only be moved independently with the declination screw. The compass needle rests on a pivot and is free to turn whenever the compass is moved.

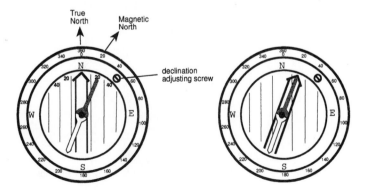

Fig. 3.2: Magnetic declination set to 0°. Fig. 3.3: Magnetic declination set to 20°E.

There are several things to notice about the orienting arrow in figure 3.2. It is pointed to north on the rotating dial. It is parallel to the meridian lines, and it is pointing to zero on the declination scale. In this example, the rotating dial is pointing to true north. You can see that magnetic north is to the east. A screwdriver is being used to turn the declination adjusting screw.

Figure 3.3 shows that the declination adjusting screw has been turned sufficiently to point the orienting arrow to magnetic north. The orienting arrow points to 20° east on the rotating dial. The declination scale is redundant but it is closer to the orienting arrow and is useful because it is easier to read than the bearing markings on the rotating dial. The orienting arrow is at a 20° angle to the meridian lines but is now parallel to the compass needle.

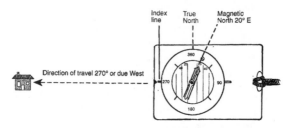

Fig. 3.4: With magnetic declination set to 20°E, the bearing of the house is found to be 270° (or due west).

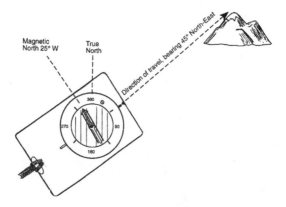

Fig. 3.5: With magnetic declination set to 25°W, the bearing of the mountain is found to be 45° (or northwest).

In figure 3.4, the base plate is added. You can hold the rotating dial stationary and turn the base plate 360°. The direction of travel is the direction of the compass bearing: either the bearing of a landmark or the bearing of the place we want to go. The bearing is read off the rotating dial at the "index line." In this example our bearing is 270° which is due west. Figure 3.4 shows an eastern declination. Points in western North America would have an eastern declination. Figure 3.5 shows a western declination as would occur in eastern North America. This is a west 25° magnetic declination and our direction of travel or bearing is 45° or northeast.

BEARINGS

The compass in figure 3.4 has a bearing of 270° and in figure 3.5 it is 45°. Bearings can tell you where you are or how to get where you want to go. You can use land features or information from a topographic map. The cardinal rule is to know where you are at all times. This means to begin each hike by knowing where you are on the map. Be aware of your bearing at all times, observe topographic features and be sure that they bear the correct relationship with where you think you are on the map. Don't wait till you get confused or lost to start checking your position.

When following trails compare the intended bearing with the bearing of the trail you are in fact traveling. If they are not the same, you are either off the trail or on a different trail altogether. Trails make travel easier but if you know your bearing you do not need a trail and are free to roam wherever you choose. The following are two techniques to establish the proper bearing to follow using information from the map. Each assumes that you know where you are on the map and have set the declination.

ORIENTING THE MAP

This technique is not the most elegant but it is the easiest to understand. You will want to master this before progressing to the next technique: orienting the compass.

Begin by turning the rotating dial until north or 360° is at the index line. Spread the map on a level surface and place the compass on the map. Align the compass base plate lengthways along the left or right edge of the map. This will make the base plate parallel to a line of longitude shown on the map. Now turn the

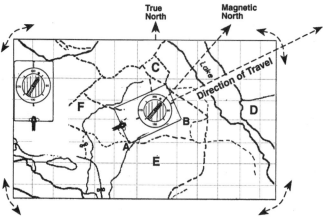

Fig. 3.6: Orienting the Map Technique; the compass is set to true north and the map is turned so as to be aligned north/south.

map and compass together until the compass needle is aligned with the orienting arrow. The map is now oriented north/south exactly the way the ground is. If you are standing at the bottom edge of the map at position A in the map , everything should make sense. Location C at the top of the map is ahead of you; location E is behind you; location D is to the right and location F is to the left. Any direction on the map will be the same on the ground. This is a quick way to figure out a lot of landmarks. If for instance, you are on the summit of a mountain, you can orient the map and quickly identify many of the peaks that surround you. If you want to find the bearing to take to go from A to B, put the side of the compass parallel with the direction A to B. Align the orienting arrow with the compass needle again, and read off the bearing at the index line. In our example the bearing is 60°.

ORIENTING THE COMPASS

This technique is easier than orienting the map but it is less intuitive. This technique does not require that the map be oriented in a north/south direction. The orientation of the map is irrelevant; the compass needle and direction arrow are also ignored. What we do need are grid lines on the map and meridian lines on the compass. If the map has no grid lines you can draw a north/south line through A.

Ignore the compass needle and don't bother orienting the map. Place the side of the compass parallel with the direction of travel

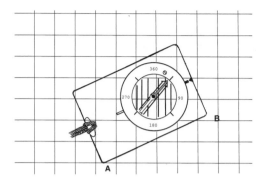

Fig. 3.7: Orienting the Compass Technique; the meridian lines of the compass are aligned with the north/south grid lines of the map.

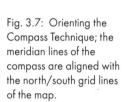

on the map. While holding the compass base plate in this position, turn the rotating dial until the meridian lines are parallel with the north/south grid lines. Read the bearing at the index line. It will also be 60°.

This technique uses grid lines rather than lines of longitude. The declination which you have set in the compass is for the angle between magnetic north and the lines of longitude (or true north). A small error has been introduced since the grid lines are at a slight angle to the lines of longitude. The difference is well within the margin of accuracy of a hand-held compass, and you can either ignore the discrepancy or reset the declination to be the angle from magnetic north to grid north.

FOLLOWING A BEARING

Either of the above techniques can be used to set a compass bearing. The bearing is the number on the rotating dial nearest the index line. The "direction of travel arrow" points the way. Cheap compasses and orienteering compasses do not have sights. The latter are intended for taking bearings quickly rather than precisely. Neither is suitable for wilderness travel. Choose a compass with sights.

Figure 3.8 shows a compass equipped with a folding cover. There is a mirror for sighting on the underside of the cover. After the bearing has been set the compass is held at eye level. The compass needle is viewed indirectly by looking at its image in the sighting mirror. The entire compass is turned until the compass needle is parallel to the orienting arrow. Observe the compass needle to be sure it is swinging freely. If the compass is tilted, even slightly, the compass needle will bind and the reading will be in error.

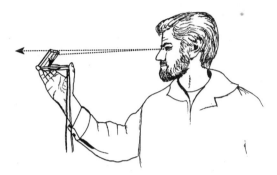

Fig. 3.8: Finding a bearing by using a compass with a mirror and folding cover.

When the compass needle is in the proper position, lift your gaze slightly and look through the sights on the top of the compass cover. What do you see through the sights? If you chose the bearing of a nearby mountain, the mountain peak should appear above your sights. If at high elevation looking for a river, you may see it below your sights. As you begin to hike and change elevation you will lose sight of these land features. There may be forests or ridges to obscure the view. Usually you will not see the objective at all, only some intermediate landmark. In a dense forest you may not be able to see more than a few hundred feet. In a fog you may not see that far. Look through the sights and select an objective which is on the desired bearing. It may be a log, a tree, or a rock. Try to pick something distinctive so that you will be able to recognize it as you travel along and view it from different perspectives. Once you get to this objective, stop and take another bearing, and pick another log or tree as an objective. When the land becomes more open you can pick objects which are farther away, and you won't have to take bearings as frequently.

DEAD RECKONING AND BACKBEARINGS

So long as you know where you started from and what your bearing is, you should be able to estimate your position. If the bearing is 60°, then your destination will still be at 60° (unless you have passed it by). Your starting point will be 180° opposite your bearing at 240°. I don't usually carry a watch when I am in the city but I always do when I am in the bush. The watch will allow you to estimate a position by dead reckoning. Check your watch frequently during the day. Estimates of time can be wildly inaccurate when hiking. A hard tough slog can seem to go on forever, while time may fly when hiking and chatting with a friend. Check your watch before you start on any bearing. If you have traveled an hour at an average speed of 2 miles (3 km) an hour, then your position will be 2 miles (3 km) along a line drawn at 60° from your starting position. You can find this position on the map and look about for topographic features to confirm the new position. If your starting position is visible, use a backbearing for confirmation.

There are two ways to do a backbearing. You can change the bearing on the compass by 180°. The 60° bearing to your destination would become a 240° backbearing to the starting position. I do not like to change the setting on my compass while I am still following a previous bearing. I am afraid of error and leave the setting alone until I get to a known position. For this reason when I take a backbearing, I simply let the compass needle go the opposite way. If the south end of the compass needle is pointing in the direction of the orienting arrow instead of the north end, I have effectively taken a bearing 180° opposite to my main bearing. This is a backbearing and does not require adjusting the compass. There is no danger of accidentally resetting the wrong bearing because I have not changed it.

If able to take a backbearing, you will probably find that you have wandered slightly right or left in the course of your travel. Now is the time to adjust course to compensate for the error. If you have been veering to the right of the intended bearing, try veering to the left. In very heavy brush, it is difficult to travel in a straight line or find unique objects to use as intermediate objectives. All the trees begin to look the same once you start to move, and the tree which you intended to travel towards will blend in with the surrounding foliage. Doing backbearings is time consuming but in heavy brush, fog, or driving snow where visibility is poor, they protect against error. If traveling with another person, use each other as a sighting object. The lead or point person takes a compass bearing and begins to walk out along it. The reference person remains behind at the position where the bearing was taken. The point person continues along the bearing line as far as possible while still being visible. He will then take a backbearing by sighting on the reference person who is easier to sight because he stands out from the brush. A colored jacket stands out against a green background. If the point person has moved off the bearing, he can correct himself with the backbearing. Once he is sure the

point person is on the bearing the reference person can move up
to the position of the point person and the point person can continue on the bearing. The process will repeat itself until visibility
improves, and the distances between sightings increases. Ideally,
the reference person will also have a compass and can guide the
point person from the last position. The reference person will watch
the point person move out along the bearing and direct him to
veer right or left.

AIMING OFF OR DELIBERATE ERROR

A few years ago, I heard the story of a white man and several Inuit
who were traveling together by dogsled. They were crossing a large
frozen lake in a snowstorm and were far from shore. There were
no landmarks and visibility was only a few feet. No one had a compass but only the white man feared being lost. The Inuit rode along
on their sleds kicking the snow every once in a while. After several
hours, they completed the lake crossing then turned along the
shoreline to the safety of their camp. The white man had no idea
how the Inuit had found their way. The Inuit had used local weather
knowledge along with a bit of "aiming off." They knew that the
wind had blown the snow into small ridges which paralleled the
shoreline. This snow lay under the fresh surface snow and by kicking away the top layer, they could feel the ridges with their feet.
This gave them the general direction they needed to cross the
lake, but once they had crossed the lake they wouldn't know
whether to go right or left to their camp. They had therefore, decided to deliberately cross the lake at a point that they knew would
miss their camp and strike the shoreline to the east of it. When
they crossed the lake, they didn't even try to head directly for their
camp. They knew the chances of striking the shoreline at exactly
the place where their camp was, were slim. By aiming away from
their camp and hitting the shoreline to the east, they were certain to find their camp by following the shoreline west. If the
white man had used a compass, he would have followed the same
route. With a hand-held compass, the white man might have come
closer to hitting the far shore at the right spot, but the prudent
thing to do still would be to deliberately aim off from the camp.

Hikers can find large topographic features with ease — there is
usually no problem finding a lake or mountain ridge. As the hiker
gets closer to his objective, he can correct for obvious error. For

the most part, lakes are down and mountain ridges are up and rivers flow downhill and end in either other rivers or lakes. There are slopes and landmarks on the horizon to guide you as you get closer. But what about a cabin located somewhere along a river? If the cabin is at a point where the river meets a lake or a tributary you set a bearing directly for the cabin. If you miss the cabin, follow the river to the point where the river intersects the lake or tributary. But what if the cabin lies along a nondescript section of the river? If you come out of the bush at the river, do you go upstream or downstream to find the cabin? If the cabin is hard to find, we are better to follow the example of the Inuit. Take a bearing which you are confident will take you either upstream or downstream of the cabin. Once you get to the river, you will then know whether to walk upstream or downstream to find the cabin.

TRIANGULATION

In the previous discussion, one started from a known point and used a bearing and dead reckoning to estimate the position. The map was used to set the bearing. To confirm the position or establish it in the first place, you will use topographic features that you can see to take bearings. This assumes you can identify and see known topographic features and they are marked on the map. Hopefully, you will see two topographic features and be able to identify them on the map. Ideally, you can take the bearings of three topographic features.

Sight through the compass at a topographic feature which is on the map. While keeping the feature in the compass sights, turn the rotating dial until the orienting arrow is parallel to the compass needle. Read the bearing at the index mark. In figure 3.9 you have obtained a bearing of 70° for a mountain peak and 110° for a small lake. You now locate the mountain and the lake on the map and reverse the procedure you followed in obtaining bearings from the map: either orienting the map or orienting the compass.

To orient the map, turn the rotating dial to 360°. Place the side of the compass along the north/south grid lines of the map. Turn the map until the compass needle is parallel to the orienting arrow. The map is now oriented north/south. Reset the compass to the 70° bearing. Hold the edge of the compass against the mountain peak and use the compass as a ruler to draw a bearing in pencil through the mountain peak. Follow the same procedure using a 110° bearing and drawing a pencil bearing line from the lake. If you extend the pencil lines, you will find that the two bearing lines will converge at point C.

Alternatively, use the orient-the-compass method. Set the bearing of the compass at 70°. Orient the compass so that the side of the compass passes through the mountain peak and the meridian lines are parallel to the north/south grid lines. Use the side of the compass to trace a pencil line through the mountain peak along the bearing. Repeat for the 110° bearing from the lake. Extend the pencil marks till they converge at point C. You have triangulated the position using two reference points and your calculated position is C.

In figure 3.9, I have shown a railway track. The railway track is a third land feature, and there is no calculation error in establishing its position. If you have calculated the position while standing near the railway tracks, you are not at point C. You are somewhere

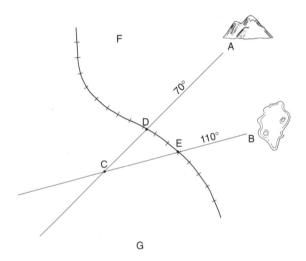

Fig. 3.9: Triangulating a position using two reference points plus a railway track.

between D and E. Double-check your work. The angle between C and B and C and A is only 40° so the margin of error is large. Ideally you would have a second reference point at 90° to the first reference point. A reference point near F or G would be ideal because it would reduce the margin of error. Check the reference points. Is it possible that you have confused the mountain or lake with some other ones? Are they in the right position relative to each other? Are the contours of the land you see as they are on the map? All of this is another way of asking yourself if the bearings make sense.

In practice this process of establishing position is not textbook simple. There may be different opinions as to which land feature is which. Rarely do we get a view of mountain peaks and can often only guess at their exact position from a lower elevation. The lake may turn out to be a pond or a wide section of river. If traveling in totally unfamiliar country, you will want to consider many different factors; some of them will support your conclusions and some may not. This is the time to discuss your reasoning with your companions. No one should accept the opinion of the "expert." The expert in the group should be able to explain his reasoning to everyone's satisfaction. You may reach a tentative conclusion. If you are where you think you are on the map, consider what land features you should encounter on the next bearing. How long should you travel before encountering this land feature? If you don't encounter that land feature in a given period of time, the tentative conclusion was wrong. If you find the land feature, the conclusion has been confirmed.

YOUR FRIEND THE COMPASS

The importance of wearing one's compass at all times cannot be over-emphasized. It should not be kept in a pocket or pack. Most compasses come with a stout cord attached. The cord is meant to go around your neck. Wherever you go during the day, the compass goes with you. My compass goes on with my hiking clothes and off with my hiking clothes. It is on when I leave the car at the start of a hike, and thereafter goes on in the morning before I leave the tent and comes off in the evening when I go into the tent. My maps are either in my pocket or in a pouch at my waist. Either way the map is easily available. There are many accounts of mountaineers being caught without their compasses. After all, they are above treeline most of the time and route finding is usually obvious. When they take off their main pack for the push to the summit, the compass can be left behind with the pack. If the weather closes in near the summit, the land features which were obvious hours before are hidden and route finding is by guesswork. Mountaineers have died of falls or from hypothermia when they lost their way and couldn't get to the survival gear in their packs. A hiker has more opportunity to get lost and an even greater need to keep his compass with him at all times.

If the compass is around your neck, it will always be with you. It is available in seconds to check on a bearing. You are more likely to use it often if it is always at hand rather than stashed in a pocket. It is also unlikely to become lost. The cord of the compass should be just long enough for you to take a bearing with the cord still around your neck. I have become slightly farsighted over the years and have replaced the original cord with a longer one. Try the compass out. Can your eyes focus on the compass in order to take a bearing or do you need a longer cord?

4.

NAVIGATIONAL AIDS

THE TIME FACTOR

The majority of recreational hiking and camping is done in summer but it is during the winter when the hours of daylight are more limited that most search and rescue operations are conducted.

Most of us turn on the light switch without thinking about it. In our homes there is no need to be aware of the setting sun and the exact hour of darkness. We do not pay attention to this daily event. Every day the time of sunset changes slightly: in the northern hemisphere there is a cycling between June 21st, the longest day, and December 21, the shortest. The dates of the equinoxes (March 21 and September 21) and the solstices (June 21 and December 21) may vary from year to year by one day. Time changes caused by Daylight Saving Time adds further complexity. Hikers should know when the sun sets. If you don't, look for it in the daily newspaper. When traveling many miles north or south to start on a hike, remember that the time for sunset will be different at a different latitude. While checking sunset time, also check the phase of the moon. This information is usually in the newspaper near the detailed weather forecast and it also appears on most calendars. On a clear night a full moon provides a surprising amount of light. I do not advocate hiking at night but it is nice to know that the extra light is available in the event of an emergency. You may have enough light to travel across open ground or along a roadway. When in camp, you will be able to walk about without a flashlight, but don't count on sorting through your gear or finding lost articles until morning.

In open areas there is a small amount of daylight before the sun rises as well as after sunset. The amount of extra light will vary with the season as well as the latitude. In the forest this light is usually marginal. Unless you have paid particular attention to light conditions of a recent nightfall, it is best to regard sunset, the time that the sun goes below the horizon, as the absolute end of the hiking day. As a hiker, you are not likely to see the horizon. In valleys, the sun will be cut off well before sunset. In the forest, the trees will block the sunlight when the angle of the sun is low, again, well before sunset. Add dark winter clouds and you will be in darkness well before official sunset. On a day hike, be sure everyone in the group knows and agrees to the time objective. What time should the hike be over? It is expected that everyone will be at a place of safety by this time. If on a multi-day hike with tent and sleeping bag, you can be more casual. The decision becomes a question of when to camp. Most of us have passed by good camping spots because it was too early in the day to stop. Hours later, we would settle for a spot half as good. With fatigue and night approaching, our minimal acceptable standard for a camping spot goes rapidly down.

Once you know the time you intend to be out of the bush, it is time to decide when to start the hike. How long is the hike? How fast will your party travel? Are there trails? What condition are they in? Will there be route finding problems? What is the fitness level of the weakest member? Do you like to "stop and smell the flowers" or are you a gung-ho group who like to put on the miles? Now add the safety factor. What if someone twists an ankle and slows the group? What if you make a route finding mistake and lose time backtracking? You now have an estimate of the number of daylight hours you require to complete this hike. Can the hike be done in the time available?

If you are going to be squeezed for time, make adjustments at the start of the day. What time is sunrise? Get this information from the newspaper. Will you have enough time if you are standing in your hiking clothes with your pack on your back at the trailhead when the sun comes up? This is the maximum available daylight hiking time. Still not enough?

Sometimes a two day hike can be finished in one day. On a two day hike you are encumbered by tent, stove, and sleeping bag. The extra weight slows you down. Setting up camp the first night and breaking camp in the morning the second day all take time. Set up and tear down must all be done in precious daylight hours which could be used for traveling. An alternative is to consider starting the hike in darkness. What are trail conditions like at the start of the hike? Usually the first few miles of a trail are beaten down and the easiest to follow. What are the physical capabilities of the group? If there is a full moon, you may have sufficient light. A flashlight or headlamp is a good backup. If you run into route finding problems you can wait for sunrise to sort them out because you have a full day ahead of you.

During the day you will have a watch available for estimating position by dead reckoning and for calculating the hours remaining until darkness. If parties split up and go to explore different areas they can agree on the time they will meet again. If only one party has a watch, coordination becomes difficult. In the bush, I have found that time is always more relevant than distance. In extremely dense bush with a full pack, it is possible to put in a full day and cover only 2 miles (3 km). The same time and effort on a level trail could result in a 20 mile (33 km) day. When Europeans came to North America, they noted that the Indians measured distances by the number of "sleeps." Hikers are wise to follow this example and think in terms of time spent on the trail.

SUN DIRECTION

Just as a sailor is always aware of wind direction a hiker should be aware of the position of the sun. The Tropic of Cancer and Tropic of Capricorn are two parallel lines of latitude which, between them, contain all points on earth where the sun is ever directly overhead. In the lower 48 states and southern Canada, the sun is never directly overhead. The exception is Hawaii which is south of the Tropic of Cancer so the sun can be overhead or slightly north in summer. From any point on the globe, the sun will appear to rise at dawn in the eastern half of the sky and set in the western half. The compass is the basic route finding tool for the hiker but the location of the sun remains a very important aspect of route finding.

On a particularly strenuous solo hike, I can recall hiking back towards the road and my vehicle. There was fresh snow on the ground, making the trail difficult to follow and I had lost my way several times and was forced to backtrack and circle about each time to pick it up again. I had been traveling for 10 hours. Finally I came below snow line and was traveling on an easy, well marked trail. I was traveling south and I started to relax as I hiked. My mind began to wander to other thoughts and I forgot about route finding. What could go wrong? I was on an easy trail and would be back at the car in an hour or two. Suddenly I realized the setting sun was straight ahead of me. The sun does not set in the south, I knew that in my location the sun sets in the southwest at that time of year. Something was wrong. There was a trail I didn't know about and I had taken it by mistake. I had not noticed a fork in the trail and had taken the wrong turn. I was so confident of my route that I had stopped checking my compass until the position of the sun roused me from my thoughts.

Be aware of the sun's position at different times during the day and the path it traces across the sky. Check the position for yourself at your location. The path the sun takes climbs higher in the sky for half a year and reaches its highest point on June 21st. It then rises progressively further south each day until it reaches its lowest point on December 21st. The more northerly the latitude, the closer to the horizon will the path of the sun be.

The location of the rising and setting sun on the horizon can also give a rough approximation of position. The following table, contributed by Professor Jayme Matthews of the Department of Physics and Astronomy at UBC in Vancouver, BC., lists the azimuths or compass bearings of the sun at sunrise and sunset for dates throughout the year at various northern latitudes. The azimuth is the angle (in degrees) measured eastward from due north. Hence, O° represents due north; 90°, due east; 180°, due south; and 270°, due west. It's worth remembering that on the days of the vernal and autumnal equinoxes (near March 21 and September 21, respectively), the sun will rise due east (90°) and set due west (270°).

The table is calculated based on a perfectly flat horizon and the times at which the sun's center crosses that horizon. Since the real horizon will often be far from flat, one must be careful when using this table in the field. The azimuths listed will be only a rough guide, but should approximate within 10° to 20° in compass bearing. If completely lost and about to spend a night in the

Latititude	20°N		30°N		40°N		50°N		60°N	
	rise	set	rise	set	rise	set	rise	set	rise	set
Jan 1	114	245	117	243	120	239	127	232	141	219
15	112	247	114	245	118	242	124	236	136	224
Feb 1	108	252	110	250	112	247	117	243	126	234
15	103	257	105	255	106	253	110	250	116	244
Mar 1	98	262	99	261	99	260	102	258	105	255
15	92	268	92	268	92	267	93	267	94	266
Apr 1	85	275	85	275	84	276	83	277	81	279
15	80	280	79	281	77	283	75	285	70	290
May 1	74	286	73	288	70	289	66	294	59	301
15	70	290	68	292	64	295	60	300	50	310
Jun 1	66	293	64	296	60	299	54	306	41	318
15	65	295	63	297	58	301	52	308	38	322
Jul 1	65	294	63	297	59	300	52	307	38	321
15	67	293	65	295	61	298	55	305	43	317
Aug 1	71	289	69	291	66	293	61	298	52	308
15	75	285	74	286	71	288	68	292	61	299
Sep 1	81	279	80	280	79	280	77	283	73	287
15	87	273	86	273	86	273	85	274	83	276
Oct 1	93	266	93	266	93	265	95	265	96	263
15	99	261	100	260	101	258	103	256	107	253
Nov 1	105	255	107	253	108	251	112	247	119	240
15	110	250	111	248	114	245	119	240	129	230
Dec 1	113	245	115	245	118	241	125	235	137	222
15	115	245	117	243	120	239	128	232	142	218

Fig. 4.1: A bearing can be determined by using the position of the sun and the time of day.

wilderness, note where the sun sets. The sun sets in the western half of the sky and rises in the eastern half, south will therefore be halfway between the two.

To use the table, take your current latitude and date and inter-polate between the values listed.

As long as you are north of the Tropic of Cancer, at latitude 23.5° north, at noon, standard time, the sun will be within 15° of due south. The exact position of the sun at noon will depend on precise longitude and whether daylight savings are in effect or not. The one hour difference between standard and daylight savings time will cause a difference in sun direction to the east of up to 15°. If you are at the center of your time zone and use standard time, the sun is exactly south at noon. If you are on daylight savings time, the sun will be directly south at 1 pm.

There are some popular navigational techniques which do not work. The old adage that moss always grows on the north side of a tree is false; moss will show up on all sides of trees. Some authorities claim that you can use a watch to find south. Point the hour hand at the sun and south will be midway between the hour hand and noon. Sometimes this works and sometimes it doesn't. Do not rely on either of these methods.

THE NORTH STAR

The North Star, or Polaris, has guided travelers since ancient times. This star is positioned within 1° of the celestial north pole. Visible throughout the northern hemisphere, its position always marks north. Throughout the night the other stars appear to move as the earth turns. The North Star is fixed above the north pole. During the year the other stars appear to change position at night as the earth revolves about the sun but the North Star continues to maintain its position.

At the north pole, the North Star is directly overhead at 90° to the horizon. It marks the latitude of the north pole — 90°. At the equator the North Star is on the horizon at 0° to the horizon and indicates the latitude of the equator — 0°. At every other point in the northern hemisphere, the altitude of the North Star marks the latitude of the observer. If the latitude is 55°, then the North Star is 55° above the northern horizon. This illustrates why this is such an important star for navigation.

If the night is clear, the North Star is a reassuring presence. It is part of the handle of the Little Dipper and is brighter than the rest of the stars in the handle. The stars in the Big Dipper are brighter than those in the Little Dipper, making the Big Dipper more easily located. Those unfamiliar with the night sky may mistake the stars of the Pleiades cluster for those of the Little Dipper.

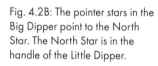

Fig. 4.2A: The position of the North Star remains constant although the Big Dipper moves throughout the year.

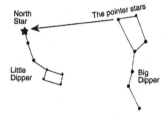

Fig. 4.2B: The pointer stars in the Big Dipper point to the North Star. The North Star is in the handle of the Little Dipper.

It is a good idea to confirm the position of the North Star by checking its position relative to the Big Dipper. There are seven stars in the Big Dipper. The two stars furthest from the handle are the pointer stars. They mark the direction of the North Star. The seven stars of the Big Dipper make an arc 25° long. The distance from the last pointer star to the North Star is a bit longer at 28°. You can estimate the 28° arc with an outstretched arm. Your fist is approximately 10° wide so the distance is almost three fist lengths.

ALTIMETER

In theory, an altimeter should be of enormous help in establishing position. Look at the altimeter and read the elevation. Check the map's contour lines. You will expect to be somewhere on the appropriate contour line. It should work in the same way as knowing you are on a river or a road. Just take a bearing off a single reference position. Where the bearing crosses the contour line will be your position.

Unfortunately, using an altimeter is more complicated than

that and requires some understanding of how they work. An altimeter is a kind of barometer, and as such measures air pressure. Although true barometers are calibrated in units of air pressure: kilopascals or inches of mercury, altimeters are calibrated in meters or feet above sea level. When air pressure increases, the elevation reading of the altimeter goes down. It may change from an elevation reading of 1,640 ft (500 m) to 1,312 ft (400 m) even though the altimeter has not moved. If the altimeter has been moved to a lower elevation, then the weight of air above it is greater and it will also record a lower elevation. The trick is to try to figure out which changes in reading are due to weather changes and which are due to changing elevation. Air pressure and, therefore, altimeter readings, are affected by movement of high and low pressure zones, temperature, and humidity. A temperature change can occur from taking the altimeter out of a warm pocket to read it in cold air. The altimeter should be reset as often as possible to try to eliminate weather factors. At the start of the hike check the elevation on the topographic map and set the altimeter to this elevation. During the hike whenever you get to positions which you can identify on the map, read the elevation on the map and reset the altimeter to the correct elevation. If camped at an unknown elevation, take steps to compensate for the weather changes to the altimeter reading that will occur overnight. If you have an altimeter with a rotary dial you will be able to set the reference point line to the elevation reading at the time you arrive. The next morning you can note the new elevation reading. If for example, the elevation has increased 164 ft (50 m) overnight, then set the altimeter back 164 ft (50 m) to where it was the night before.

Watches with altimeter functions are available at reasonable cost. They have digital readouts and no pointers. In this case keep an altimeter log. Record the evening altimeter reading and compare it with the morning reading. Add or subtract the difference before you leave camp.

Experienced mountaineers should anticipate

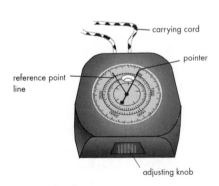

carrying cord

pointer

reference point line

adjusting knob

Fig. 4.3: The altimeter.

the possibility that rapidly changing weather conditions will obliterate distant landmarks. They will take the time to correct their altimeters whenever they are at a known elevation and weather systems are changing. They are likely also to spend the extra money to ensure that they have reasonable accuracy. For hikers, the decision to use an altimeter is a personal one. My own experience with altimeters has not been good. I have noted overnight reading drops of 820 ft (250 m). What if this drop had occurred during a hike? If my last known elevation was 10 hours ago, the reading on my altimeter would have been in error by 820 ft (250 m). And what about altimeter error? One particular search and rescue operation sticks in my mind. The victim had been missing for several days and was assumed to be hypothermic and unresponsive. The search was conducted in rugged mountainous terrain where it was all but impossible to hold a straight compass bearing. We conducted our search using altimeters. After adjusting the altimeters to the same setting we spread ourselves down the mountain slope. We walked parallel to each other maintaining a separation of 33 vertical ft (10 m). One would have expected atmospheric pressure to effect the altimeters equally so that we would continue to walk parallel to each other. In fact teams converged and diverged and their paths intersected. The different error factors in each altimeter made for lots of confusion. Don't expect accuracy. Each individual altimeter reading should be considered accurate to within 33 or 100 ft (10 or 30 m). The less you pay for the altimeter the less accurate will be the reading.

If you are about to buy a new watch you may decide to pay extra money for a combination altimeter/wristwatch. Are you hiking in steep terrain where an altimeter is useful? If you hike in level country with few contour changes, the altimeter may not be much use. Are you prepared to go to the trouble of resetting the altimeter during the hike? If altitude readings are important to you, you have another option: a Global Positioning System.

GLOBAL POSITIONING SYSTEM

The Global Positioning System, or GPS, is a technological breakthrough in navigation. The GPS receives signals from satellites orbiting the earth. The position of these satellites at any given time is known. The GPS contains an accurate clock and can triangulate on the satellite positions to determine the location of the

GPS. The GPS can give a readout of its position in either grid coordinates or latitudes and longtitudes (lats and longs). If the GPS receives signals from four satellites, it can also provide elevation in either feet or meters. The elevation reading is much less accurate than the location reading.

GPS technology was first used by mariners. At sea there are no obstacles to block the satellite signals from one horizon to the other. Models for commercial trucks driving city streets and highways followed. As weight and cost decreased they have been used by mountaineers and other outdoor enthusiasts. Mountaineers travel at high elevation above treeline without a forest to screen out signals. Hunters and fishers like to have the ability to identify favorite places for a return visit.

The GPS has some obvious advantages over the traditional map and compass. A compass position is determined by triangulating from known landmarks and topographic features which are visible. At night, in fog, or during snowstorms no compass sightings are possible. The GPS, however, can receive satellite signals regardless of visibility or atmospheric conditions. There are, however, situations where the hiker will have problems using a GPS. The satellite signals must reach the GPS. In a valley these signals can be blocked by mountains or signals may bounce off mountains causing error. Trees and forest canopy can reduce and restrict satellite signals. GPSs vary in their sensitivity and the degree to which signals can be blocked from reaching the GPS antennae.

Locations can be stored into memory or taken from a map and programmed into the GPS. The capability of the GPS will depend on the particular software program. A list of locations in the memory can be plotted on a map or seen on a digital display to show the route taken. Some systems can store maps in digital form to be used for route finding. These GPSs will have locations preset. The user can also take the coordinates from a map and input the GPS. When in motion, the GPS will be registering locations along the way and will indicate on the screen if the user has varied from the proper bearing.

A compass will continuously point the bearing direction regardless of whether the compass is moving or not. A GPS records only a series of locations. When the GPS is stationary there is no way for it to continue to reliably indicate direction of travel. The bearing will, however, be displayed in degrees, so that a compass can be used to sight the bearing. When the user moves far enough from his first position, a second position can be recorded. The GPS can then be used to determine if the second and subsequent positions are in line and tending towards the target.

It is rare that one moves in a straight line through the bush. Rivers, cliffs, and gullies all conspire to throw us off our bearing. When using a compass you must guess how far you are being forced to deviate from the bearing. After passing the obstacle, one must try to compensate and regain the original bearing. If you can't see a reference point to take a backbearing, you are just guessing the distance necessary to get back on the bearing. The GPS has the advantage that it will identify how far you have moved from the proper bearing and let you know when you have correctly returned. The GPS can also provide the speed of travel as well as the estimated time of arrival at the target location.

Altimeters measure air pressure and errors in elevation readings arise from weather and temperature changes. The GPS is not affected by these variables. GPS technology does have limitations when measuring elevation. It measures elevation with far less accuracy than it measures position.

It would be a mistake for hikers to consider the GPS to be a replacement for a compass. A GPS is larger and heavier than a compass and much more expensive. They run on batteries and have the same problems as all electronic devices — they work only as long as the batteries maintain their charge. Batteries do not work well at low temperatures and neither does the LCD (liquid crystal display) screen. No electronic device likes rough handling or moisture. Snap off the antennae, drop the GPS on a rock or into a puddle, and you'll be taking it back to the store for repair or replacement. Always carry a compass to fall back on, they are easy to use and almost indestructible. A compass uses no batteries and lasts forever. By all means use a GPS but don't forget a compass.

PHONES

Adults who take teenagers on hiking trips are often surprised and amused by the unusual items that turn up in their packs. On a week-long trip on the West Coast Trail on Vancouver Island, I found one student with a cellular phone. This was years ago when cell phones were much bigger and heavier. Needless to say, cell telephone service was not available. They are not a reliable emergency communication system for hikers. I have tested cell phones in the mountains north of Vancouver. In some areas they work well. On the top of nearby Golden Ears Mountain, one can sit on the summit at an elevation of 5,600 ft (1,706 m) and look down at the city. You can see the city but you can't phone there. The cell phone may be useful in or near urban areas but is of no use in wilderness areas where there is no cell coverage

We would all like Dick Tracy's watch. Long before cordless telephones were invented this comic strip character had a telephone in his wristwatch. We are still a long way from having Dick Tracy's watch. Mobile satellite communication systems are in use which overcome some of the cell phone's limitations. Like the GPS, they rely on satellites. They have the same limitations as GPS in that the satellite signal can be blocked by mountains and trees. They are too expensive for occasional recreational use at this time and are much bigger and heavier than cell phones. They are a phone in a briefcase. Mobile satellite telephones will be of interest to those establishing a base camp in the bush. Carry them by truck, packhorse, Skidoo, or canoe but not on a human back.

PERSONAL LOCATOR BEACONS

Like telephones, Personal Locator Beacons (PLBs) do not assist in navigation. They are a way of communicating. PLBs are capable of sending a distress signal via satellite technology to search and rescue authorities. At the time of purchase, the owner's particulars are recorded and registered with the authorities. Light and small enough to be carried, the PLB is transported in an off position. During an emergency the antennae of the PLB is raised and it is turned on. The distress call is received at the search and rescue monitoring station, and the location of the PLB is noted. The identity of the user is obtained and search and rescue response is immediate. Currently locations can be pinpointed to within .6 to 1.8 miles (1 to 3 km) so visual contact with the victim is still important. They are an expensive piece of equipment but are available on a rental basis from some dealers. They weigh a couple of pounds with batteries.

5.

ROUTE FINDING

The compass, along with an appropriate map and the knowledge to use them, are the equipment common to mountain climbers, hunters, backcountry skiers, snowshoers, and outdoor enthusiasts of all descriptions. The best navigators will have difficulty in holding a straight course in thick forest. There is a built-in bias to select the easier way. If the land is sloping, we will tend to favor the downslope and veer in that direction. The most experienced person can make errors in route finding, but it is the compass which minimizes those errors, helps in discovering those errors when they occur, and puts the traveler back on the proper route again.

This chapter will assume that the reader has read and understood the previous chapters on maps, compass, and navigational aids. It is assumed that the hiker is carrying a topographic map, compass, watch, and has a general idea of the path of the sun through the sky.

WHERE TO HIKE

Where does the idea for a hike come from? Like most hikers I carry a list of trips in my head that I would like to do. Sometimes I even write them down — a wish list. It is amazing that no matter how many hikes I do, I can never get to the bottom of the list! In fact, I am falling behind. No sooner do I go on one hike than

several others suggest themselves. What lies in the next valley or
along the other trail? If I meet someone on the trail, he will inevitably tell me about some trip that I have not done. Sometimes I do
one trip and add three more to my list.

A major source of trip ideas are the regional trip guides found
in hiking supply stores. Check the stores for your area; is such a
trail guide available? Government park authorities publish bro-
chures describing individual parks, and references to trails crop
up in newspapers and magazines. Sometimes, a reference in an
article provides the name and place of a person that you can track
down and make enquiries of. Fishermen won't tell you where their
favorite fishing holes are, but hikers love to talk about where they
have been. I collect and save hiking trip ideas. It has been said that
you can find out anything you want to know in six phone calls.
Usually not that many are required. Years ago I came across a book
of local history that described the unsuccessful settlement of the
northern part of Vancouver Island — 'The Cape Scott Story."[1] I
began to wonder if it was possible to retrace the old telegraph line
route which the pioneers had strung through the bush. A few telephone calls gave me enough confidence to try the route. My wife
and I were dropped off by float plane at the furthest point and we
took a week to hike out. It was not until the fourth day of hiking
that I noticed a twig broken along the route at pack height; my
first indication that humans had recently passed that way. A little
bit of research can get you off the beaten track and away from the
crowds.

Often just staring at maps can rouse your curiosity. If there is a
small lake on the map, what is it like? How could you get there? If
there is a mountain, can you hike up it? How far does a trail go
and what is at the end? There is no limit to the possibilities. If you
can use a map and compass you can put your finger down anywhere on the map and go there. Then there is the joy of discovery.
Old blazes in trees mark a route to where? An old mine — a min-
eral claim — perhaps a prospector's cabin — or an abandoned
farm. I used to canoe on a large lake near Powell River in British
Columbia. I noticed another lake near it on the map but could
see no trail to it. One weekend, I paddled to the end of the lake
and took a compass bearing over to the new lake. What a delight-
ful weekend: exploring the country, finding a lovely lake, and
poking about an abandoned cabin.

Trail guides are not a substitute for a map. Ideally the trail guide will describe those landmarks observed and noted by its author at the time the author traveled the trail. As a practical matter the author will probably not have traveled all the trails himself but will rely on other sources which may be old or unreliable. I have seen trail descriptions which were just plain wrong. Missing information may be just as dangerous as wrong information. You may be traveling the trail and unexpectedly confront a junction in the trail. If a map or trail guide does not describe the junction, how will you know which way to go? Do you take the trail to the right or the one to the left?

Landmarks themselves may have changed. I recall hiking along a route described in a trail guide. I came to a T-junction and took the route to the right. I was quite confident that this was correct: it was the proper bearing and the topography was right. But the trail guide said I would be turning right at a logging road at this point. Where was the logging road? After a while it dawned on me. The species of tree on the trail was different from the surrounding trees. Although my book was reasonably new, the information sure wasn't. Back in my grandfather's day this route may have been a logging road but it wasn't any more. The logging road had grown in and become a trail.

Trail guide maps can also be misleading. Use them by all means, but carry a topographic map and use it as a back up. Check to see where north is in the trail guide map. Do not assume that up is north. Often sketches will be oriented to best fit the page. Maps in canoe river guides can be even more confusing. The maps are in the largest possible scale so as to identify all the many places referred to in the text. This means multiple maps on multiple pages. No sooner do you get used to the map on one page and the general direction of north than you turn the page to the next map and find that north is somewhere else.

With a topographic map you can depart from the route shown in a trail guide. A topographic map will orient a hiker to the whole area and permit unrestricted movement in this larger area subject only to natural barriers.

Topographic maps have contour lines and therefore describe the hike in three dimensions. Trip guide sketches rarely do. Occasionally, the trip guide will be a photocopy of a topographic map, but without the color markings of the original topo. I find this confusing too. Rivers, contour lines, trails and lakes are all the same color — black. If you can sort it all out without making a mistake by all means do, but again, carry the topographic map as a backup.

I find carrying a trip guide in a book awkward. Books don't fit into pockets, they go in packs — and that isn't a convenient place. My solution is to photocopy the page I need and leave the book at home. It is easier on the book that way and the single page from the book can go in a resealable plastic bag and then in a pocket. That way the page is dry and protected.

HIKING CLUBS

Hiking clubs are an excellent source of trip ideas and with the increasing popularity of recreational hiking, clubs are becoming more numerous all the time. If you don't know of a hiking club, a little detective work may be in order. Hikers usually have other outdoor interests: skiing, cycling, canoeing, or mountaineering. Ask at other clubs. Talk to hikers, ask at outdoor supply stores, or contact environmental or wilderness preservation groups.

A hiking club is a repository of an enormous amount of local knowledge. What is the best time of year to do certain trips? What level of fitness is needed for particular hikes? What is the scenery like? How long will the trip take? Experienced members of the club will prepare a calendar of hikes — a hiking schedule, and ensure that there is a leader for each hike. The trip leader will plan the trip. Where will everyone meet? What time? Are there special instructions? Those wanting to go on the trip will register for the trip. If insufficient interest is shown in the trip by the cut-off date, the trip will be cancelled. If weather conditions turn bad, the trip leader will decide whether to cancel the trip. The trip leader will expect all participants to sign a waiver, releasing both the trip leader and the club from legal liability. When on the trail, the trip leader is the boss, but you are ultimately responsible for your own well-being. Take a map and compass so you know where you are and have enough survival gear to be self-sufficient. Then relax, enjoy the trip and let the leader make the decisions. Next time you could be the trip leader, so make life easy for him. If you say you will go on the trip, you have made a commitment. If you are late everyone will be waiting for you. For safety and liability reasons the club may require a minimum number of participants. If you don't show up on the day of the hike, the trip may be cancelled and everyone sent home. Make life as easy and pleasant as possible for the trip leader because it is sometimes hard to get them. Keep with the group. Do not get too far ahead or too far behind. It is bad form to leave the group but if some unforeseen circumstance arises, discuss it with the trip leader. If you do decide to leave the hike, the trip leader should have another person as a witness to verify that you are leaving the group and that the group will no longer be responsible for you.

TRAILS, BLAZES, AND ANIMAL TRAILS

A trail is a logical sensible thing. A highway may follow the route of an old trail, but there the similarity ends. Most roads begin their lives in warm, dry offices as lines drawn across maps. They are conceived by politicians, planners, and consultants. They usually avoid private land boundaries, conform to budgetary constraints, and respond to political pressure. They are built through bogs, under avalanche chutes, across rivers and are cut into mountainsides. They are not natural and do not fit the land. Bad trails are built the same way. They are an imposition on the land.

Before Europeans came to this continent and brought with them horses, the native people roamed the continent on foot and by canoe. When traveling by canoe, they followed well-known portage routes which were essentially short trails. The repeated passage of humans kept the brush from growing back and made the portage route discernible. Samuel Hearne accompanied a group of Natives on a two year overland journey. His trip took him from Hudson Bay to the Arctic Ocean. Alexander Mackenzie took the Grease Trail across the western mountains to the Pacific Ocean in 1793. These journeys were on trails which existed because they were the best way to cover the distance. The Grease Trail, now preserved as the Alexander Mackenzie Heritage Trail, was an artery of commerce. It is 215 miles (347 km) long and takes 21 days to travel in one direction. These trails existed without planners, consultants, politicians or maintenance budgets.

With the introduction of axes it was possible to easily chop out a bit of bark from a tree at eye level and the blazed trail was born. The bark does not grow back and the blaze is as permanent as the tree. If you see blazes in the bush ask yourself where they go and how old they may be. One summer day I followed a blazed trail near one of the deep inlets on the west coast of Vancouver Island. It was fun to follow, wondering as we did where the trail of blazes would lead.

We guessed that horses had been used on the trail as it cut slightly into the slope. At the end of the blazes we found an abandoned mine where some hardy person had made a camp and driven his adit the hard way: with shovel, hammer and hand-held bit.

The distinction between animal trails and trails for human hikers is a tenuous one. There are not two separate networks of trails: one for people and one for animals. In fact, many hunters know that the best place to see game is along a road. The road hunter cruises the backroads with gun beside him. If the hunting pressure is low, he is most likely to see game from the road and has a short carry. His sporting fellow hunter can push through the brush all day, his rewards will be fewer. The animals choose the easiest route. If there are no humans about, they will follow roads and trails. Both humans and animals will walk around a bog rather than through it and both will avoid cliff faces. Humans, like animals will choose the path of least resistance. All traffic conspires to leave its mark although the hoofed animals are more damaging to soil than the human boot. Moose are giant, heavy animals and their repeated passage can leave a trail well-marked. Horses are the real bulldozers. A packtrain of horses following each other in single file are real trail makers. Over time they wear steep-sided trench-like trails through the bush. In damp areas their great weight kills the plant life and turns the trail into bog.

If hiking in a wilderness area, in all probability you are hiking on an animal trail. The real question is whether the trail is going where you want to go.

Trails do not run straight; they swing back and forth, constantly changing their course to avoid difficulties and seeking the best route. The general direction is the trend of the trail when all the swings back and forth are factored out. Where does the trail seem to be going? Why does the trail skirt a difficulty to the left rather than the right? The overall direction of the trail is its bearing. If the map tells you that you should be moving to the northwest and that the correct trail also trends to the northwest, be sure to check your compass periodically to be sure that you are still going in the correct direction. Be aware that for most locations, if your general direction is west, the sun should be on your back or left shoulder in the morning, and front and left shoulder in the afternoon. If your general direction is south, the sun should be to the left during the morning, in your eyes at noon, and to the right in the afternoon.

CHOOSING THE CORRECT TRAIL

On heavily traveled trails near urban centers, the dilemma is not finding a trail but finding the correct one. Where there are multiple trails, it becomes difficult to show them all on one map. Map makers must be selective and maps will not show all trails. Trails may have been added or re-routed since the map was made. The hiker will frequently come to a point where the trail forks either to the right or the left with no indication of which is the right one. Your map may tell you that there is an intersecting trail ahead, and your route will take you on the left branch. How will you know when you are at the correct intersection? There may be other intersections with other left turns. If a hiker has been checking his map and compass along the way, he will have a general idea of his position and of the general bearing of the trail he must take. The new trail must be tested with a compass. Go along the new trail to determine its general bearing. Is this the bearing of the trail you are seeking? Does it go northeast? If it does not go northeast, you are on the wrong trail. Be sure to follow the trail far enough, until positive of its bearing. It is just as important to be sure that it is the wrong trail as to be sure it is the right trail. If you give up too soon, the trail may make another turn to a different bearing. Suppose this really is the correct trail. You only followed it for a short distance before it established its true bearing. If you gave up too soon, you will go back to the main trail and start testing other branching trails. You will eventually find out these other trails have the wrong bearing too. By then you will be confused, emotions may be rising and you will waste a lot of time before you come back to test the correct trail a second time. When assessing a trail's general direction, be aware of routings due to land features. A trail may go east to avoid cliffs, a bog, or to find a river crossing, then swing west after passing these features to establish its true bearing.

When testing trails and routes, be very cautious about leaving your pack behind. No one likes to haul a heavy pack anywhere it doesn't need to go but you will be much more uncomfortable should you be separated from your pack. If you do leave your pack behind take a minute to clearly identify the spot, and make sure you can easily find it again. Many a canoeist begins to shuttle his gear in stages across a portage, then returns for the next carry to the frustration of not being able to find his gear. I will share my embarrassing moment. I had been intrigued by the moss-covered remains of a wooden skidway through bog and heavy brush. One day I traced this old route and found the remains of an old cabin and stables. In an earlier day, loggers had used horses to haul cedar shakes from the area. I was delighted by my find and spent a few hours exploring. Eventually I grew thirsty and reasoned that the cabin had to be near a water source. I put down my pack and headed downhill. I knew a lake lay in that general direction. My reasoning told me that cabins are always close to water — it wasn't. I went further and further taking no note of my bearing or landmarks. When I tried to get back to my pack I had a big problem. An old cabin in heavy brush can be like a needle in a haystack. That is what had protected it all these years. Taking out my compass, I took a trial bearing from the lake — no cabin, no pack. Back to the lake and follow a different bearing — still no cabin and no pack. Back and forth I went, more disgusted with myself each time. With only a few hours of good daylight left I gave up, left my pack in the bush, and hiked out. The next day I retraced my original route to claim my pack.

FALSE TRAILS, POOR TRAILS, AND NO TRAILS

At some time you may become frustrated with the route a trail is taking and want to take a "shortcut" off the trail. Resist this temptation. A trail is an indication of the consensus of bush travelers as to where the easiest path should be. They have literally voted with their feet. If there were an easier, more direct way then that would be the trail rather than the trail you are standing on. Remember that you can travel far faster and more easily along a trail than through the underbrush. Several miles of backtracking along a trail to a different trail will probably be quicker and easier than the "shortcut."

Sometimes one encounters false trails that peter out and end nowhere. Every footfall in the forest damages vegetation and leaves marks of its passing. A party of hikers may miss a turn in a switchback or try a shortcut unsuccessfully. By the time they have returned to the trail, they have created a false trail by traveling the wrong way twice and left marks of their passing. Another party may make the same mistake, this time encouraged by the broken and crushed vegetation they will press on further than the first party thereby extending the false trail. In time the wrong way becomes a short trail leading nowhere.

Geologists, forestry workers, surveyors and others all use colored

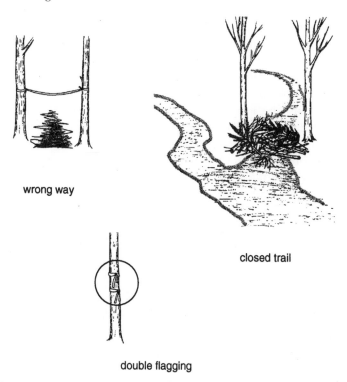

wrong way

closed trail

double flagging

Fig. 5.1: Wrong Way: The incorrect route is blocked with flagging.
Closed Trail: The trail has been rerouted and the old trail blocked with cut branches.
Double Flagging: This signals an abrupt change of trail direction, an intersecting trail, or a corner post where flagged grids intersect.

plastic tape or "flagging" in the bush. Many hikers use flagging when they are off trail. This means that there are thousands of miles of flagged routes which have no official sanction and are not meant to be a guide to hikers. The purpose of the flagging and the direction of travel may only be known to the person who put it there. Flagging does not necessarily lead to safety and may end abruptly. Trail builders mark proposed routes with flagging. As they become more familiar with the terrain, they may add flagging elsewhere where they find better terrain. Ideally all the extra flagging would be removed but some may remain.

If following a good trail which turns bad over a short distance, it is best to stop rather than to push on. Check your general compass bearing and landmarks; perhaps go back along the trail to a point you are confident about. Have you inadvertently turned off the main trail or are you following a false trail? If the trail has been "adopted" by a local hiking club, they will attempt to block the false trails by placing brush across the point where they leave the main trail. Occasionally, trails are re-routed to avoid mud, fallen trees, etc. and the trail builders will try to block the old trail section with brush. Be aware of brush in the trail and if it appears to be placed deliberately or the ends are sawn or cut, do not automatically move it to improve the trail.

When feet become fewer, trails are less distinct. A greater degree of route finding skill becomes necessary. The trail becomes more subtle. Route finders place flagging along the route. Plastic flagging tape hardens, breaks and falls to the ground. It should be placed to one side of the trail where it will not be damaged by being brushed against by packs. Often, it is put on the same branches that hikers will grab to steady themselves and is quickly knocked loose. Some is placed on dead branches which will inevitably break off and fall. Some flagging is placed too low and is hidden by snow or is difficult to see from a distance. Some is placed on one side of a shrub so that it is only visible to hikers following in the same direction but becomes invisible from the opposite direction. Flagging can be hard to see and loses its bright original color over time. Cheap flagging may lose its color and become white. Whether faded to a white color or purchased as white flagging, it will be equally hard to see against a background of snow. Yellow flagging may blend with sun on autumn leaves and even the pinks and reds become hard to see in heavy brush. After a season much of the flagging will be gone and there will be holes in the trail. When following a flagged trail it is essential to know your compass bearing to facilitate traveling between the unflagged holes in the trail. Abrupt changes of trail direction frequently cause difficulty. Most trail builders will signal a change in trail direction by double flagging the last flag at the point where direction changes. If you come to double flagging, don't assume that the trail continues in the same direction. For all these reasons following a trail of flagging can be challenging.

POINT PERSON SYSTEM

It is recommended that the lead hiker travel well in front of the second hiker. The lead hiker becomes the point man. He keeps going as long as he has more flagging in sight but stops at the last flag he can see. At that point he should shout back to the second hiker that he has "no flags." The second hiker then stops and looks back to check the general direction of the flagging. By indicating the general direction of the flagging to the lead hiker he can assist the lead hiker to see the next flag. By maintaining their separation each person can view the bush from a different perspective. If the point man knows his compass bearing, he can take a back sighting with his compass using the second hiker as his reference point. He can then move left or right to position himself along the proper bearing and look ahead in the direction flags are to be expected. If the direction of the flagging has not changed he should be standing on the trail. He may discover the missing flagging on the ground or signs of the passage of other feet. If there is no sign of passage the point man can move to the right or left of the general direction searching for flags, and the second man can move up and search the other side.

The decision to pass beyond the last flagging should not be taken lightly. One spot in the bush will very quickly look like another. When traveling in one direction, it is instructive to turn once in a while and look in the direction from which you have come. The route will look different from the opposite direction. It is quite possible that you will not recognize the route. The absolute prerequisite for continuing into the bush is a map and compass and route finding skills. What is your general compass bearing? What are the general topographic features through which you are passing? Do you recognize them and your position on the map? Is there a road, a river, or a valley or other large feature which you expect to encounter? How difficult is the terrain? If you make a mistake and veer to the right or left of the proper path, how will you know you have made a mistake and what will you encounter? How much time should pass before you encounter a recognizable topographic feature? A good trip leader will ensure that every member of the group understands these factors and feels confident to proceed. If you are dependent on finding flagging to get to your destination with confidence it is probably better to turn back now and take a better-known route.

DISAPPEARING TRAILS

Finally, I would like to caution you about what I call disappearing roads and trails. I met my disappearing road when I was nineteen and the lesson has stuck with me ever since. Three of us had traveled along a logging road to a trailhead. The trail led away from the logging road and then turned parallel to it. We followed the trail to our destination which was a geologic drill site which was being used for taking geologic core samples. My buddies turned to go back along the trail the way we had come. Being the foolish one, I decided that since the trail was traveling parallel to the road, I would take a shortcut directly to the road through the bush. I figured I'd be back to the road before they were. They took off down the trail and I went on my shortcut. After an overly long period of time and distance I began to wonder where the road was. I knew my direction was correct, but why wasn't I intersecting the road? Eventually I heard a truck and could tell by the sound where the road was. It was, of course, my buddies driving up and down the road looking for me. Between me and the road was a narrow pond which blocked my way in both directions. I swam the pond and emerged on the road soaking wet and a little wiser. I learned two things. The first was that trails are located where they are for very good reasons. This trail went the long way back to the road so people didn't have to swim across ponds. The second item of information was even more important.

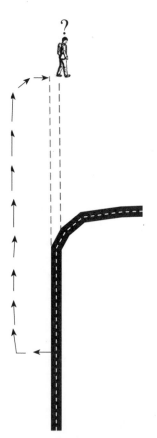

Fig. 5.2: The disappearing trail.

If you are traveling parallel to a trail or road don't assume that the road or trail goes in a straight line. There is no law that says it will do this. How often do we drive along roads without really seeing the twists and turns?

Kevin Young encountered his disappearing road under more stressful circumstances. He planned for a day of hunting in northern Alberta near a seismic road, constructed by an oil-exploration company, and arranged to be dropped off on the road in the morning and to be picked up further along the road late in the day. His friends would drive along the road and find him wherever he happened to be. After being dropped off, Kevin headed directly into the bush and soon intersected an animal trail which appeared to run parallel to the road. The trail made travel easy and he spent the day following it. Late in the day he set a compass bearing to take him back to the road. He left the trail and cut through the bush to the road.

After a while, Kevin realized that the road was not where he thought it would be. It had disappeared. With night falling, should he keep traveling forward, perhaps circling towards where the road might be? Should he go back part way along the trail, then gamble that he was adjacent to the road and try again? Should he go all the way back the way he had come and risk spending an unplanned night in the bush? He chose the latter course and by traveling at top speed, he was able to arrive at the road before nightfall.

---

1   Peterson, *The Cape Scott Story*

6.

HIKING
TECHNIQUE

WATER CROSSINGS

On a Saturday in January four hikers left for an overnight hiking trip to Widgeon Lake, near Vancouver, B.C. The lake is a popular destination for both day hikers and overnighters but canoe-only access to the trailhead keeps the number of hikers down. The four rented a canoe from an outfitter and left to paddle up Widgeon Slough to the trailhead. The hike to the lake would take three or four hours. When darkness fell on Sunday, the outfitter became concerned because the hikers had not returned. When he went to investigate, he found only the empty canoe at the trailhead. But where were the hikers?

The police were duly notified. They, in turn, contacted the Coquitlam Search and Rescue Team and the Provincial Emergency Centre authorized a search. In the early morning hours of Monday a mobile command center was put into position, made operational, and two ground search teams were taken to the trailhead by inflatable raft. Another search had begun. I sat in the command vehicle listening to the wind and the occasional radio communication from the search teams. The rain had finally stopped. Finally at 4 am came the news. The first search team were on the trail but the trail was blocked by water: a stream. What should they do?

It became clear what had happened to the missing hikers. They had left Saturday morning and there had been heavy rains Saturday, Saturday night, and early Sunday. The trail to Widgeon Lake was a good one but I did recall a place where water run-off crossed the trail. Sometimes that place was dry and sometimes there were a few inches of water flowing. The recent heavy rains would change things dramatically. A few inches of gentle water flow would become a few feet of raging rapids. The hikers had spent a wet weekend at the lake, watching the rain. They did not realize that the rain waters were building into torrents and those torrents had closed the trail behind them. They were, in a sense, marooned at Widgeon Lake. They had no way to escape until the floodwater lessened and the trail opened up again.

This story is not unusual. Rising water levels will often cause difficulty and should always be considered when planning a hike. The topographic map will show where the major watercourses are but there may be other smaller watercourses not marked on the map. Some streams only flow in spring when snow melts or when heavy rains fall. The greater the area being drained, the more water will collect and need to drain away. Rocky slopes or valleys which have been logged will drain quickly and dramatically. They lack soil and vegetative cover to hold the rain and release it gradually. If there are streams, how will you get across? Most of us pick good weather for hiking. This means that we cross streams when they are their gentlest and at their lowest levels. If you are on a multiday hike the weather can change after your hike begins. If unlucky, you may be facing a few surprises. Streams may become unrecognizable in a different season or after heavy rains. Channels which were dry, fill up with water. Streams which one can rock-hop across may become serious fording challenges. Streams which can normally be forded with rolled-up pant legs may become impassable.

The north country has innumerable lakes and rivers. How did the original inhabitants travel overland in the great wet lands that now form the Northwest Territories? The writings of Samuel Hearne describe how Natives traveled great distances across forest, tundra, rivers, and lakes. On December 7th, 1770, he began a hike which would last 18 months, 23 days, and cover 2,200 miles (3,500 km). Almost all of his journey was across land no European had ever seen. Hearne walked across unmapped forests and tundra with his Native guide Matonobee. He became the first European to see the Arctic Ocean above North America. His journey started at the Hudson Bay trading post, Prince of Wales Fort, near present-day Churchill, Manitoba. He traveled mostly east to Great Slave Lake, then north to the Coppermine River and the Arctic Ocean. By traveling in winter conditions Hearne and his party were able to walk across frozen lakes and rivers including Great Slave Lake. Knowing they would encounter summer conditions above the treeline, Hearne's party built a few small boats in the forest which they carried with them. The boats were used to cross lakes and large rivers which could not be forded. Hearne reached the Arctic Ocean on July 7th, 1771, and immediately turned back. He traveled through a second winter before reaching Prince of Wales Fort on June 29, 1772.

In 1988, Dutch outdoorsman Bart de Haas hiked solo from the Arctic Ocean west of the Mackenzie River Delta across much of the Yukon Territory and into British Columbia. Many streams lay in his way. Sometimes he would find someone to ferry him across by boat. At other times he would be quite alone. Bart carried plastic and rope for these situations. An 80 pound pack is difficult to handle in the water. Bart wrapped a few things at a time in plastic to waterproof them. He then tied the waterproof package with one end of the rope and looped the other end around his neck. As he swam the streams the current would wash him a distance downstream. Bart would walk back up the far bank before swimming back for the next load.

Shore Belay

Few of us have the grit or self-confidence of a Samuel Hearne or a Bart de Haas. We certainly do not plan to cross streams which cannot be forded. There are however, times when a crossing must be made even though the water is so treacherous that there is a possibility of being swept off one's feet and risking oneself and one's gear. Mountaineers will know exactly what to do. They would ford such a river using a rope and a shore belay. One member sets up a belay on the near shore, ideally anchored by several wraps of the rope around a tree. A loop is formed at the other end of the rope and goes around the torso of the tallest and strongest, passing under his arm pits. The person fording may find that the line catches on rocks in the river and becomes a hazard. It is, therefore, important that the person crossing be able to slip quickly and easily out of the loop if he chooses to. It should be loose around

Fig. 6.1: The bowline knot.

the body and the knot should be fixed rather than sliding. A bow-line knot is fine.

The belaying party feeds the rope out until the person fording reaches the far side of the river. The rope itself can be a problem since it will drag in the current and pull on both the anchor and the person crossing the river. Any extra rope will belly in the current and add further drag. Ideally, there will be sufficient rope so that the party fording can angle downstream to the current. This minimizes rope drag. It also results in the anchoring person being able to bring the rope taut to help steady the swimmer against the current. Finally it results in the swimmer traveling a shorter arc should he lose his footing and be swept back to shore. After the line is fixed in position on both banks, the whole hiking party and their gear can cross in relative safety.

Foot Entrapment

The ultimate hazard in river fordings is drowning, usually caused by foot entrapment. Foot or leg entrapment is also a hazard for canoeists. A canoeist pitched from his canoe is no different than a hiker who loses his footing while fording a river. In rivers with fast-flowing water, it is natural to attempt to stand and resist the current of the water. If there are large rocks in the river, the feet can become jammed against and between rocks. A struggling person can easily lodge his feet between rocks and be unable to reposition himself so as to extricate his feet. If the person stumbles, his upper body will likely fall in a downstream direction. While pinned by the foot the water will rush over his body. The force of the river will prevent him from getting up again or raising his head out of the water. Even in thigh-deep water, the water can rush over a person, keep his head below water and drown him. Be careful where you put your feet. The rule if you are swept off your feet is to not try to stand up. Float on your back. Move your head upstream and your feet downstream. This will protect your head from crashing

Fig. 6.2: Drowning by foot entrapment.

into rocks and debris and you will be able to see better downstream. Backstroke diagonally upstream and work your way slowly to shore. This is a called a ferry. Do not attempt to stand until your buttocks hits the riverbed. This will indicate that the river is approximately knee-deep at which point the chance of leg entrapment is reduced.

Tripod Crossings

The tripod is a good fording and river rescue technique. It is based on the assumption that three people together will be stronger and more stable than one. Three people face each other forming an equilateral triangle. Each person grabs the other two people firmly. As they work their way slowly across the river there are six legs instead of two to hold the group in position. Between them they have three times the strength to resist the power of the river. If anyone stumbles, there are two other people to steady him. If the river can't be crossed with the combined strength of three people, it probably shouldn't be attempted.

River Fording

Take time to assess where the best fording place is; the shallower the better. The trail may not lead to the best fording place. Most people hike in the summer and in good weather and if water levels are low, there may be no reason for them to consider other places. There are several indications of shallow water. If river speed is constant at two places: one part narrow and one part wide, then the wide part will be most shallow. A narrowing in the river will mean the fording is shorter but the water will be deeper. A fast portion of the river will usually be shallower than a slower portion of the same river. Water rushing over a gravel bar will be shallowest of all. Beware of undercut banks, particularly on the outside of curves. Water does not move at the same speed everywhere in the river — it follows the easiest path between two points. When water encounters a bend in the river, it accumulates and pushes against the outside bend. This force causes the outside of the bend to be eroded and even undercut. It also means the current is faster and the water deeper. When looking for a place to ford a river, be cautious of undercut banks. An undercut bank means the river is eroding the soil and vegetation and this usually indicates deeper water with strong currents. The inside of a bend is usually slower water where silt is being deposited and the river is shallower. You may be fortunate and find a section where the river braids or divides into two or more channels. Usually the individual channels will be shallower and slower than the main river.

When river crossings are to be expected, it is a good idea to take camp shoes along. Walking across a rocky river bed can be difficult to do, particularly in bare feet. If you slip on the rocks, even sandals may not protect tender feet. Water distorts the view of the river bed so your feet do not always go where you intend. The current pushes the feet and the body in a downstream direction. Cold temperatures of northern rivers and glacial streams can be painful.

If your boots are dry, it is best to take a few extra minutes to safeguard them. Take them off and store them safely in your pack rather than carrying them in your hands or tying the laces and letting them swing around your neck. If you do stumble in the river, you can use your hands to save yourself while keeping your boots out of harm's way. Consider what would get wet if you fell in the water and your pack were submersed. Is your sleeping bag wrapped in a plastic garbage bag? Put on your camp shoes (running shoes will do fine) and proceed slowly.

When a fording is necessary, sticks are usually available when needed along the river bank and need not be carried. Your stick should be straight, strong, and about shoulder height. If the current is strong, it will become a third leg and your safety will depend on it. Remember to plant your stick on the upriver side of your body. If you plant your stick on the downstream side, the river current will have a tendency to carry the bottom of your stick away from you. On the upstream side, the current acting against the bottom of the stick will push the stick down firmly into the stream bed.

Fig. 6.3A: Correct upstream stick placement.

Fig. 6.3B: Incorrect downstream stick placement. Refraction causes the hiker to misjudge the position of the rock.

Refraction can cause hikers to misjudge where to put their feet. Light bends at the water surface. If you are looking at an object in the water from an angle, it will not be exactly where it appears to be. Fording rivers can be tricky. If you fall, you will at the very least get your pack wet. Slow down. Choose the crossing place carefully, get a firm stick for balance and proceed carefully and deliberately.

Rock Hopping and Foot-Stomping

At lower water levels when large rocks stick above the water surface, rock-hopping becomes possible. Examine the stream bed. Can you step or jump from rock to rock all the way across? If you step on a rock with a round bottom, it will move and you will slip off and into the water. If there is a green appearance to the rock, it is probably slippery with algae. You can go quickly and hope that if one rock moves, you can catch your balance on the next rock or go slowly, testing each rock and using a stick for balance.

If the water is only a few inches deep, it is possible to quickly stomp your way across. This is a full run with your feet landing flat and splashing the water away. A reasonably level bottom is necessary. Before the water flows back, your foot is gone and reaching to make the next splash. Using this technique the biggest danger of wet

Fig. 6.4: The running foot stomp.

feet comes not from the foot doing the splashing, but from the following foot which is coming forward just as the water is being splashed. To avoid this, bring the following foot high and to the side to avoid it being splashed.

Even on muddy trails water can seep between the sole of your boot and the upper. A waterproof welt, the material stitched between the sole of the boot and the upper, is important. Many boots now come with a synthetic waterproof welt. For those which don't, boot sealers are available to waterproof this vital joint.

Running Jump

The running broad jump crossing provides a laugh for onlookers when the jumper doesn't jump far enough. It is amazing to me how many hikers overestimate the distance they can jump. Not surprising when we consider that no one gets much practice jumping in hiking boots with a weight strapped to their back. My most embarrassing jump happened when no one was around to see me except my dog. The snow was several feet deep and was cut by a small stream which had not frozen. The banks were piled high with snow. The stream was only a couple of feet across. I came to a stop next to a snowbridge across the stream. My dog walked across and stopped to stare back at me. I wondered if the snowshoes I was wearing would displace my weight enough for me to use the snowbridge. If the dog could make it across, maybe I could too. Not true. No sooner had I started to test the bridge than it collapsed, pitching me forward. I ended up with shoulders and head on the far side of the stream and feet and snowshoes on the near side. My middle was suspended between snowbanks, a few feet over the water and sagging badly. I was immobilized and unable to release my feet from the snowshoes. To add insult to injury, my dog thought this was some new game I was playing for his benefit and came back to lick my face and bark at me. I was about to become very wet and very cold.

Log Crossings

Fallen logs over streams form the worst and best of bridges. The best of them are the fallen forest giants. If they are slightly rotten on the upper side, so much the better. The soft decaying wood makes the top surface flat or slightly concave and provides good traction. Branches sticking out from the trunk can be used for handholds or to lodge the sole of the boot against for extra stability. Rounded logs are best crossed with toes pointing to the sides and feet splayed out. If the heel of the boot is to one side of the midpoint of the log and the toes are on the other side, there is greater purchase on the log.

The larger logs can be crossed on all fours. It is hard on the knees but if there is a long drop, play it safe. If the log is too small for crawling, try the leg straddle. Put one leg on either side of the log and sit down facing the far end of the log. Put your hands in front of you on the log and rock forward putting your weight on your hands. Pull your body along the log. A slow and awkward way to get across but it is the safest of all.

A log with loose bark offers the most treacherous footing imaginable. Loggers wear sharp steel caulks projecting from the soles of their boots to afford traction on slippery logs. If the caulks do not penetrate through the bark and into the tree itself, the log will still be slippery. Even bare logs can be treacherous, particularly if there is a greenish or wet coating to the log. When walking along logs, keep the chest and hip straps of your pack unfastened. If you fall, you will be able to fall clear of your pack. Falling with a pack often means your upper body is weighted and you may be falling head first. The weight of the pack increases the severity of injury. The added weight may mean your arms will not be strong enough to catch hold of a branch or to break your fall.

PACE

Husband and wife, parent and child, or even regular hiking companions are unlikely to share the same preferred hiking pace. In a large group with different abilities the people in front become impatient with the laggards at the back. People become separated, and communication breaks down. Ideally, thought should be given to this issue at the outset. Maybe the group should be split into two groups: a fast group and a slower one. How often will there be rest stops? Who will lead the group and set the pace? Who will be the last person and stay behind the stragglers? When parents hike with children, the pace should be the pace of the slowest child. This can be frustrating for the parent who wants to "get there," but can be an important way to teach a child to appreciate the joys of nature. One way of doing this is to put the child in control. The child can be the leader, get to carry the watch, and decide how many minutes there will be between stops.

In large groups there is the possibility of the laggards getting further and further behind until they lose contact with the rest of the group. The least capable may become lost. Large groups should designate a lead person who is familiar with the trail and a sweep who is also an experienced hiker who can maintain a position to the rear of everyone else in the party.

The smaller the group, the more likely it becomes that everyone will be traveling at close to their own pace. But what is an ideal pace?

An ideal pace is one which can be maintained over the whole day. Most hikers start off too fast. The leader doesn't want to slow people down, the group is fresh and raring to go, and so they all speed along the trail. A stop after fifteen minutes to take off a layer of clothing is to be expected. But how much exertion is best? If sweat is running down your face and your clothing is getting soaked from perspiration, the pace is too fast and you will be forced to stop soon. This stop and go type of hiking is agonizing for everyone. In winter conditions, it is even more important to reduce the pace to avoid the clothing becoming wet with perspiration. If someone is panting hard, the pace is too fast. The outer limit of the group's pace is the fitness level of the weakest hiker. Exceed that limit and the whole group will be stopped. Any gain made from pushing the weak members faster will be more than offset by the time lost at stops.

Experienced hikers intuitively know what their ideal pace is for all kinds of terrain. The pace is more a level of expenditure of energy than of speed. When terrain steepens, the stride shortens and the tempo slows but the level of energy expendited remains constant. Do not allow minor obstacles to break your stride, push through the underbrush rather than breaking pace. Once the body is moving rhythmically, the mind lifts away from the body and thinks of other things. Tibetan monks are said to travel hundreds of miles in walking meditations. Up ridges and down valleys they stride, lost in their private worlds. To interrupt their stride is to break the spell and return them to the discomforts of the trail. I find that I reduce fatigue by keeping a regular pace. Freed of bodily discomfort, I often surprise myself with how far I have come. Bart de Haas, a Dutch hiker mentioned earlier, favors solo wilderness hikes of up to 1,000 miles (1,600 km). He stops every two hours in the morning and every hour in the afternoon. His pace is fast and his stride is long. Over easy terrain he can cover 19 to 21 miles (30 to 35 km) a day with lots of time left over at the end of the day to make camp. Alone, there are no compromises in the pace one chooses to go. Frequent stops can be tiring as at each stop the pace is lost and must be regained. Fatigue sets in and the body complains anew, perspiration dries and the body cools, the rest stop lengthens and then it is an effort to start hiking all over again and try to regain the flow. Far better to go slowly and steadily and let the miles drift by. It is a case of the tortoise and the hare; the hare never establishes a traveling pace and rushes from rest stop to rest stop, while the tortise doggedly puts one foot in front of the other. Late in the day fatigue can be expected; the hiker who has budgeted his energy will maintain his pace. The hare will slow the group as he calls for more rests.

At the end of the day mistakes are most likely to occur. With a desire to push ahead to a cold drink or a warm car, there is a tendency to become lax in route finding and hikers are more likely to get lost. Landmarks and trails look different coming from a new direction. A setting sun changes the color of vegetation; the shadows move and grow and areas become dark which were once sunlit. It is not a time to speed up but perhaps to slow down and become more deliberate, to study the map, look for landmarks, and check the compass bearing. A tired body makes more mistakes and stumbles become more frequent. This is a time to be extra careful about foot placement.

SPEED

How far can one travel in an hour, a day, or a week? It all depends. Pace is only one factor. It accounts for the amount of physical energy you have available to expend on a sustained basis. The terrain will dictate how far you get. You may travel 21 miles (35 km) in a day over easy terrain or 2 miles (3 km) in nightmare conditions. The following table is a suggested schedule of speeds for a healthy individual carrying a full pack and traveling continuously without major stops.

Established Routes

paved roads	3 to 3.5 mph (5.0 to 5.5 km/h)
gravel roads	3 mph (4.7 km/h)
trail over rolling hills	2.5 mph (3.8 km/h)

Off Trail Bush Travel Using a Compass

flat terrain	1.4 mph (2.3 km/h)
rolling terrain	1 mph (1.6 km/h)

Mountainous Terrain

Ascending: allow one hour per 1,312 ft (400 m) of vertical distance plus one hour per 2.5 miles (4 km) of horizontal distance;

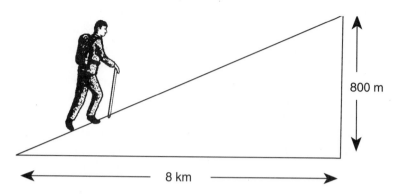

Fig. 6.5: Calculated hiking speed: 4 hours up and 2 hours 40 minutes down.

vertical distance: 2,624 ft (800 m)/1,312 ft (400 m) x 1 hr = 2 hrs
horizontal distance: 5 mi (8 km)/2.5 mi (4 km) x 1 hr = 2 hrs
                                                              Total = 4 hrs

Descending: allow one hour per 1,968 ft (600 m) of vertical distance plus one hour per 3.7 miles (6 km) of horizontal distance;

vertical distance: 2,624 ft (800 m)/1,968 ft (600 m) x 1 hr = 1 1/3 hrs
horizontal distance: 5 mi (8 km)/3.7 mi (6 km) x 1 hr = 1 1/3 hrs
                                                    Total = 2 hrs 40 mins

On a multi-day traverse with bad terrain at one end, there should be a conscious decision on which direction to go. The West Coast Trail on Vancouver Island is one such trail. The northern end has the best trail and the southern end the worst. Do you plan your trip so as to encounter the rough section near the beginning of the trip when everyone is fresh or reverse the trip and do the rough section last when you have eaten most of your food and the packs are the lightest?

LEG ACTION

Most day hikes begin with ascents and end with descents. One climbs from low-elevation valleys and roads to higher elevations which are more natural and remote. Going down, one has the advantage of height; trails can be more obvious when seen from above. A route which was hard to follow going up may not be a problem going down, unless it is a scramble down a steep rock face. On the ascent, one's face is closer to the rocks and hand and toe placements are more easily seen. Going down it is harder to see where the holds are and it is possible to miss the proper route and come to an impassable section, necessitating a climb back up to find the easier path. A rope wrapped around a tree, can be a comfort on rocky descents. If the rope is looped around a tree, the rope can be recovered by pulling on one end. Remember to consider the danger of hikers dislodging rocks onto those below. When there are loose rocks it is best for the hikers below to stay clear of the route which rocks would take if dislodged from above. Wait until those above have completed climbing that section. If this is not practical, climbers should cluster together so that dislodged rocks will not gain speed and momentum or start to bounce away from the rock face in an unpredictable way.

There is a skill to hiking. To walk along a sidewalk is a simple matter. Take away the smooth surface, add rocks, logs, mud, water, snow, leaves, branches, and a thousand obstacles and the walk becomes more demanding. There is a technique to hiking which the novice has not usually mastered. There are ways to move through the bush quickly and easily. For an accomplished hiker it becomes second nature: a way of knowing how to place the feet, move the legs, swing over deadfalls, and miss obstacles. Why does one person veer to the left around an obstacle while the novice goes to the right? Why does the novice fall more often? Why does he take longer? Why is he constantly breaking his pace? Why does he complain so much and stop so often? There is a skill to moving through brush and the heavier the brush, the more skill is required.

Good hiking technique is a collection of subtle habits. Spend enough time hiking in challenging terrain and these things are there to be discovered. Watch for the wasted effort in climbing on and off small obstacles. If there is a log across the trail the novice may step on the log then off again. The veteran swings his leg over the log without breaking his tempo. He literally takes small obstacles in his stride. When light underbrush fills the trail, the veteran tips his head forward to protect his eyes and ploughs on through. The novice will invariably stop, grab the branches and push them away with his hands.

When grabbing the branch, novices often break off a portion in the mistaken belief that they are helping to clear the trail. They are actually creating a hazard. A branch in its natural state comes to a tapered end and is padded with leaves along its length. The broken branch is a sharp object sticking into the trail ready to poke into the next hiker. Far better to leave the branch alone and push through. If branches are to be broken, they should be broken at the main stalk so that no sharp wood is sticking into the trail.

Good hiking technique means knowing instinctively where to place the feet. Step on a rock one way and the rock will roll, step on it differently and it is a wedge under the sole of your boot allowing leverage without a misstep. Wrong foot placement in heavy brush or boulder fields can do more than slow you down. Place the feet carefully to avoid foot entrapment. To lose one's balance with one's foot lodged between rocks is to risk a sprained ankle or broken bone.

Avoid jumping off obstacles when carrying a pack. Jumping with a weight on your back is hard on the body. It is better to gently lower yourself. Apart from the shock to fatigued muscles, there is the real danger of hyperextending the knee if the ground is rough. Some jumps seem unavoidable. When jumping, the knees should be slightly bent at the time of impact. To misjudge the distance or to have the footing give way and to fall further is to risk the possibility that the knees will be straight at the time of impact. The full weight of body and gear will be transmitted to the knee joint.

Bad knees are the curse of many hikers who claim that going downhill is harder than going up. They complain of pain in the legs and knees caused by the steady braking action on the descent. The problem is likely a combination of poor hiking technique and inadequate leg strength. When the downhill foot reaches out to receive the hiker's full weight, the knee should be bent. It becomes a bent spring and the impact is not felt in the knee joint but in the muscles of the leg: specifically the quadriceps. Skiers are told to keep their knees bent and hikers should learn the same thing. By building strength in the muscles of the leg, one will be able to keep the knee slightly bent. For the unfit, a bent knee may stop a case of bad knees and cause only a case of sore quads.

OLD CABINS AND HANTAVIRUS PULMONARY SYNDROME

Only bad weather would cause me to sleep in an abandoned cabin rather than a tent. Without artificial light they are invariably dark and gloomy. Shadowed from sunlight, darkness comes early and morning comes late. They are invariably dirty. If used occasionally by careless campers there is often a rodent problem. If you miss the tell-tale rodent droppings during daylight, you will surely hear the rodents themselves during the night. Emboldened by darkness they may run across you as you sleep and scurry about in the cabin keeping you awake. Food will be targeted and packs and other gear chewed and ruined. Suspending gear from the rafters by at least a foot of rope will keep belongings safe.

Added to this is the concern for hantavirus pulmonary syndrome. Although rare, this disease associated with deer mice can be fatal. Hantavirus can reside in rodent urine, saliva, and feces. If conditions are dry the virus can be inhaled in the dust from the mouse droppings. The virus may also be transferred to mouth and nose from contaminated hands.

Initial symptoms usually occur within the first two weeks. They are general and flu like: fever, headache, pain in the abdomen, joints, or back, and sometimes nausea and vomiting. The prime symptom is difficulty in breathing caused by a buildup of fluid in the lungs

7.

YOUR FEET
AND HOW TO
CARE FOR THEM

BOOTS, GAITERS, AND SOCKS

Protection and care of the feet is the third consideration in the hikers holy trinity; the first being staying warm and dry to maintain the body's core temperature, and the second is route finding and map reading skill to ensure that the hiker knows how to get home. The feet are what will carry you there and back. Sore, blistered, or bleeding feet are no fun. I have seen hikers miles from a road with large patches of skin peeled off their feet. They limp along clutching a stick or a friend's shoulder to lessen the agony of each step.

Foot care begins with the selection of appropriate boots. The type of boot required will depend on the terrain, the season, and the weight carried. Rigid insulated mountaineering boots for ice and glacier travel, heavy thick leather boots for snow travel, medium weight waterproof for multi-day hikes, and light weight fabric boots for short day hikes on good trails. The solution may be to have several pairs of hiking boots. I have three: lightweight, medium weight, and heavy weight. The lightweight are my good weather, easy travel, day trippers. On summer days, it is hot sweaty feet that I want to avoid. They are not only uncomfortable, but in the heat the skin becomes soft and more easily blistered. On easy trails with a light pack one can reasonably place comfort ahead of foot support and protection.

Medium weight boots are three-season hiking boots. A Gore-Tex liner makes them waterproof and leather uppers give moderate protection from injury. A sturdy sole protects the bottom of the foot even while carrying a substantial load. The leather offers good stiff ankle support.

Heavy-weight boots are more tiring to walk in but are the maximum in foot protection. The thick leather uppers mean one can come down uneven talus slopes with little regard for foot injury. The solid sole retains its shape and lodges into foot holds when rock scrambling. Walking on sharp rocks is not a problem — they can't be felt. This is especially a blessing when strapped into snowshoes. The traditional snowshoe has an opening for the toe and the instep pivots on a cross-member. The constant pressure of the cross-member against the instep is uncomfortable unless the sole of the boot is tough. In winter, heavy boots offer protection from the cold and their inflexible tough leather makes them ideal for kick stepping. The stiffness allows crampons to be strapped on to attempt slippery ice and hardpacked snow conditions.

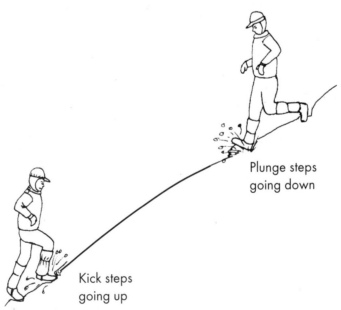

Plunge steps
going down

Kick steps
going up

Fig. 7.1: Kick steps and plunge steps are used to avoid falling on snowy slopes.

Heavier boots come at a cost. They will probably not feel as comfortable as their lighter relatives when first pulled on and will take longer to mold to the foot and are more likely to cause blisters than light boots. Once molded to the feet, however, heavy boots will be just as comfortable and will last longer and offer better foot protection. Lightweight boots may be so soft as to require no breaking in. The traditional way to break in rigid leather boots is to stand in a creek, soak the boots completely, then go for a walk. Boots with identifiable pressure points can be taken to an experienced boot repair shop where they can stretch the part of the boot which is causing discomfort.

When shopping for boots, bring the same weight of sock that will be worn for hiking. Avoid using the store's socks and certainly don't use regular-wear street socks. Compare fit by loosening the laces and shoving the toes forward in the boot. See if one finger fits between your heel and the end of the boot. Beware of buying boots with a snug fit; on a hot summer day feet will swell and fit the boots differently than they did in the store. In winter, with thicker, warmer socks the boots may be too small. Feet are insulated by the air in the boots, if extra socks are forced into the boots air will be expelled and the feet will become colder faster with less insulating air. In the wintertime, feet will be cold if boots are overly tight and the resultant constriction of blood flow can lead to frostbite.

Boots which are too big have their own set of problems. If the foot is too narrow for the boot it will slide about causing the toes instinctively to press down to arrest the movement causing a blister. If the boot is too long, the heel will shift up and down and cause heel blisters.

Gaiters are worn to prevent snow, rain, or water from the underbrush soaking the socks and getting to the feet. Gaiters can be worn off-trail to prevent small rocks, needles, and other debris from falling down into the boots causing blisters. This advantage is offset in warm weather by the build-up of heat and moisture under the gaiters and in the boots.

In snow, the gaiter is worn over the pant cuff. In this way, snow will be pushed up and over rather than under the pant leg and against the socks and skin. In wet conditions when rain pants are worn, the arrangement is reversed. If the gaiters are worn on top of the pants, rain will run down the rain pants, work its way between the gaiters and pants and soak the socks and feet. Short gaiters can instead be worn against the calf and under the rain pants; the water will not get the socks wet.

The hiker's traditional wool socks has been supplanted by a confusing range of sophisticated specialty socks. No sooner does one become comfortable with one type of sock and material than it is swept from the store shelves to be replaced by a newer model. Read the advertising, talk to other people and experiment. The ideal sock will protect the foot from rubbing against the inside of the boot; help to control moisture on the surface of the skin; cushion the foot from injury; keep the foot at a comfortable temperature; and dry quickly. Often two pairs of socks are worn. The extra cloth layer helps to absorb movement within the boot. This reduces skin abrasion and therefore blisters. The inner liner socks are thin and are of a material designed to wick moisture away from the skin and into the outer sock. The outer sock is the main insulating layer. Commonly the outer has a thick cushion where it is needed: at the heel and toe. The sock's insole is thinner and therefore cooler. It provides a good cushion even when the sock is wet, which is just as well because most socks are hard to dry on the trail.

FOOT CARE

Before the boots go on, take a look at your toenail length. Toes may be jammed forcefully into the ends of boots during a hike, particularly when going downhill and it can be very uncomfortable. Cut toenails nice and short. Carry nail scissors in the first aid kit so that on a multi-day hike nails can be continually trimmed. Additionally if there are pressure points which are likely to rub and cause blisters, try and do some prevention. The best line of defense against blisters is moleskin, manufactured by Schering-Plough HealthCare Products under the trademark Dr. Scholl's Kurotex. Moleskin has a fuzzy coating on one side. This is the side which faces the sock. The reverse has a strong adhesive. Moleskin is sold in small packages which can go directly in the first aid kit. Each package contains several 3" by 6" sheets. Mole skin should be a standard item in every hiker's first aid kit, together with scissors to trim the moleskin to size. Cut the moleskin to the exact size and shape you need before removing the glue backing. Be sure that it is large enough to cover the entire trouble spot with a small margin. Once the backing is removed, the mole skin is glued to the skin. Protect the patch from grit which can work its way into the glue at the margins of the patch and cause further problems. Be sure the edges lie flat against the skin and don't bunch up. If the patch is not firmly in place, the glue side will stick to the inside of the sock making it difficult to remove the sock without pulling on the patch. Once on, the patch cannot be removed easily. If a blister has already begun to form, the skin will be damaged or even ripped if the patch is removed prematurely: get it right the first time. Once applied, the fuzzy side of the patch receives any abrasion while cushioning the skin below. If the skin below is slightly damaged, it will heal under the moleskin. The moleskin should be left alone to work loose and fall off by itself. Moleskin is a souvenir of the hike to be worn for a week or so after you get home usually lasting through several showers. By the time the moleskin falls off, the skin below should be healthy again.

Finally put the socks on, but be sure the sock seams are properly lined up. If wearing no-heel liner socks make certain the toe seam goes on top of the toes. Toes should not rest on a seam. Turn the socks inside out and give them a shake. Be sure there is no debris in or attached to them. Then check boots for grit. Turn them upside down in case there are any insects, then feel inside to be sure there are no other irritants. Force the heel well back in the boot, then tie up the laces. Avoid over-tightening. Sometimes the laces over the instep need to be tighter than the laces at the ankle. If going downhill toes will have a tendency to jam forward into the boots. If the boots are stiff or a bit too big, the heel may rub up and down. In either case, try pushing the heel back in the boot and tying the laces extra tight along the instep. Then do an overhand knot before continuing the lacing up to the ankle. The overhand knot will allow the instep laces to be tight and the ankle laces to be looser. This should keep the toes back in the boot while keeping the ankle loose enough to be flexible.

Pull the liner socks up under the pant leg and pull the outer sock over the pant leg. This keeps everything in place and the three layers protect shins from bangs and scrapes. Grit and dirt may work its way between the socks and boots but it won't get next to the skin.

Be very careful about adding extra insoles to your boots. Sore feet are often a result of carrying a heavy pack on rough ground and adding extra insoles is not usually an appropriate solution. The extra thickness under the feet raises the spot where the heel bone connects with the boot. Boots are designed for the heel bone to be in a certain position and they have a recess to accommodate it. If you move your heel bone up and partly out of this recess your heel will rub and you will get a blister. The solution is not to wear extra insoles, but to get heavier boots with a thicker and more rigid sole which will provide more protection for sensitive feet. Light boots are fine for day hikes but not for extended jaunts with a heavy pack.

At the end of a long day of hiking it is a real pleasure to take off those heavy hiking boots and put on clean dry socks and a pair of light shoes. On multi-day trips a pair of running shoes perform very well as all-purpose camp shoes. Sandals are lighter but do not afford good protection. If you are wearing mole skin, grit will get in the mole skin. Camp shoes reduce the number of hours when boots must be worn, give boots and socks a chance to air out and dry, and are simply more comfortable to wear around camp. If the trails are easy, feet can be given a break by tying the boots on to the pack and walking in running shoes. For fording streams, camp shoes are ideal and far safer than bare feet. If the stream is rocky and the current swift, sandals are better than bare feet but are not as stable as running shoes.

Because the sensation of a blister about to form is so subtle, the novice hiker will probably miss the signal and not notice until the blister has formed completely. When hiking with new boots or when feet get hot and sweaty, it is important to closely monitor the sensations in the feet. The beginning stage of a blister will be felt as a slight burning sensation. This can be on the sole, the toes, or at the heel. If the toes are constricted they can rub together resulting in blisters between the toes. At the first hint of a problem the prudent hiker will stop and examine his feet. The problem area will be slightly red and more sensitive than the surrounding skin. Let the skin dry in the air before applying the moleskin patch. Hot sweaty feet blister easily and so keeping the feet cool and dry is important. On long rest stops, it is a good idea to take the boots off, air the feet, and spread the socks out to dry.

If a blister does form, gluing moleskin on top may not be the best alternative. Consider either Molefoam or 2nd Skin. Molefoam is similar to moleskin in that it is an adhesive sheet sticky on one side and fuzzy on the other. It is however substantially thicker than moleskin. This time the patch is cut in a doughnut configuration. The patch will be cut oversize, larger than the blister. A hole will be cut out of the patch the size of the blister. When placed over the blister the Molefoam will not contact the sensitive blister but will form a border around it. Hopefully, the blister will be small enough so that any abrasion will take place against the Molefoam and not on the blister. The Molefoam has its own glue to keep it in place but the Molefoam can be reinforced with medical tape. 2nd Skin can be used in conjunction with the Molefoam in the centre of the doughnut patch.

2nd Skin is a soft dressing which is 80% water. It comes in a sealed package to prevent it drying out. Cut the 2nd Skin to shape, peel off the plastic side and apply directly to the skin. Cover with gauze and medical tape. Because 2nd Skin is mostly water, it will dehydrate after it has been taken out of the package. If the dressing sticks to the skin, soak it in water to rehydrate it and remove. If the area of blister is confined, the doughnut hole in the Molefoam patch can be placed over the blister. Medical tape can keep everything in place. The Molefoam will keep the blister from pressing heavily against the boot.

Back home review the manufacturer's instructions for boot care and waterproofing and follow these instructions religiously. The more faithfully these instructions are followed, the longer feet can stay dry on the trail and the longer boots will last. All boots will get wet under sustained wet conditions. Leather boots are almost impossible to get dry on the trail. Put them too close to a fire and you will damage the leather and lose whatever waterproofing remains. Dry socks won't keep feet dry either — if you put dry socks in wet boots you will soon have wet boots *and* wet socks. If socks do become wet be very careful when drying them near a fire. Modern synthetics do not tolerate heat very well and will melt into a ball, cooling into crisp plastic-like material if placed too close to a fire. You can't hike with hard bits of plastic in your boots.

8.

LOST

WOOD SHOCK

Willpower, strength of character, tough-mindedness, resourcefulness — there is a quality of character which is hard to put into words, but is closely linked to personal survival once the props of civilization have been kicked away. Without it, lost hikers have died though they carried a tent and life's essentials with them. With this quality, people have survived in the face of impossible odds.

Slavomir Rawicz[1] was swallowed up by Stalin's secret police and spat out in Northern Siberia to do twenty-five years of hard labor.

He led a group of seven prisoners who escaped from prison into an arctic blizzard. Their gear was pitiful: cloth bags instead of packs, animal skins to repair boots and clothing, a bent nail and flint stone instead of matches, a knife, an axe, and one metal cup. Fear of recapture kept them away from settlements as they fled the Soviet Union and escaped through China. With no maps or compass, they followed the sun south walking 4,000 miles (6,400 km) over a one year period. They crossed the Gobi Desert going as long as twelve days without water. Then they crossed the Himalayan Mountains into India. It is remarkable, not that three died on the journey, but that four survived. Their strength was an indomitable will to live and a strong camaraderie.

Being lost has an enormous psychological impact. In fact, all lost persons suffer psychological disturbance to some degree. Syrotuck[2] states that:

> "Regardless of how well and healthy a person seems to be when rescued, there is almost always some degree of shock. Even people who while lost appeared to use good judgment with no suggestion of overt panic exhibit what we like to call "wood shock." Many persons found mobile and well, will seem to converse in a completely normal manner. Only upon close questioning does it become evident that they are unable to remember where they spent the first night, whether they had water to drink or whether they crossed the river yesterday — or maybe the day before."

Wood shock, the psychological effect of being lost, progresses in the following stages:

1. **CONFUSION:** Confusion comes with the realization that what was familiar is no longer. Initially, the hiker was traveling a route with confidence. At some point doubt began to intrude. Is this still the route? Am I on the correct trail? Perhaps I am no longer on any trail and nothing looks familiar. Which way should I go?

2. **FEAR:** Confusion leads to fear. I am lost. I am alone. When night comes I will be in the dark. Maybe I will be hurt by animals, or freeze, or starve. Maybe no one will find me and I will die.

3. **PSYCHOLOGICAL TRAUMA:** Fear and confusion can alter perception. The surroundings may seem to spin or appear to be closing in; a feeling of vertigo or claustrophobia may ensue. Victims may disrobe, removing layers of clothing needed for their survival. These items may be found by searchers, folded and stacked neatly. Hypothermia and heat stroke (discussed in other chapters) can cause irrational thoughts which may explain some of the odd behaviors exhibited by lost persons. Indeed, hypothermia may rob a person of good judgment and cause them to become lost.

4. **PANIC:** The urge to "do something" becomes irresistible and is often characterized by bizarre and irrational acts. The lost person will feel a need to run, to break free of the situation.

In his haste vital clothing or needed equipment may be left behind. Unless the victim manages to "get a grip," the physical response will culminate in exhaustion or injury. Injury can be caused by running into trees or other objects or falling. Exhaustion will then be a contributing factor to hypothermia. The depleted body is less able to withstand the rigors of low overnight temperature.

5. **DESPONDENCY:** What is the lost person's ultimate response to the knowledge that he is lost? For some it is a desire to think and act carefully, to find shelter, to light a fire, and to take all prudent steps necessary to ensure survival. For others, it is a time of helplessness and despair: tents will remain unpitched and fires unlit. A deadly fatalism overcomes good judgment.

GETTING MORE LOST

If one becomes lost it is useful to consider the predicament from the point of view of those who will be searching. Search and rescue planning begins with an assessment of the subject's destination, probable route, and likely location. Information will be obtained from friends and family. When a person first becomes lost, they are probably close to their intended route. Search efforts will certainly include that route and the area near it. If within this area, the chances of being found are excellent. The more distance traveled the more difficult it will be for searchers. Let's assume that the lost person was last known to have been at location A, but has subsequently become lost.

Let's also assume that he stopped when he realized that he had become lost and is now within one km of A. From high school math, the area within 1 km of A can be calculated using the formula πr^2 where π is 3.14 and r is the radius of 1 km. The area to be searched is therefore 3.14 square km. This represents an area which search and rescue organizations will be able to quickly and effectively search with available personnel.

Now, assume that the subject has wandered 3 km away from A. Using the above formula, the area to be searched is now 28 square km and at 10 km from A, the area to be searched grows to 314 square km. Such a large area will obviously require a much larger contingent of searchers and take considerably longer with the re-

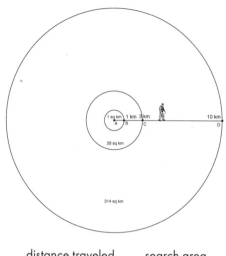

	distance traveled	search area
A to B	1 km	3.14 square km
A to C	3 km	28 square km
A to D	10 km	314 square km

Fig. 8.1: The further the distance traveled, the larger the search area needs to be. Therefore, the best place to be found is close to the place that you became lost.

sultant possibility that rescue will come too late.

The conclusion is clear. The best chance of rescue exists close to the place where one initially became lost. Resist the temptation to "do something" unless the plan has been carefully considered and discussed with everyone in the group. The tendency when lost is to travel in the direction of least resistance: to walk to a clearing or through light brush rather than heavy brush, to walk downhill rather than uphill. The path of least resistance is not necessarily the best route and walking for its own sake will not improve the situation. During good weather, studies show that lost children have a higher survivability than adults. It is believed that children simply attend to their own needs. When they are tired they rest. Adults are more likely to push on and exhaust themselves in the process. In bad weather children have reduced survivability due to their proportionally greater heat loss leading to hypothermia. Staying put, therefore, is a decision which will not, in all likelihood, make the situation worse, will increase the chances of being found relatively quickly and will conserve energy.

GETTING FOUND

The next step is to plan for basic comfort and survival. Seek shelter and light a fire. Focusing on these tasks will keep the mind occupied and help to keep the spirits up. Do all that is possible to help the searchers. Spread a tent or other material in an area visible from the air. Smoke from a fire may be visible for miles. Use the mirror of a compass as a reflector signal. If near a trail or other natural route, expect searchers to walk along it. Make a signal with branches or rocks to attract attention. Anything unnatural will be noticed: stack some rocks, arrange logs or boulders in a pattern. The more that is done to attract attention, the better the chances of being found quickly. Hypothermia will reduce one's ability to hear and call out to searchers, so use markers. Stay visible.

The main reason hikers become lost is not accident or injury but plain misdirection. Every hiker starts with a plan or objective. It is always valuable to talk to someone who has done the same hike before, but remember that one is likely to encounter decisions and situations on the trail that one was not forewarned about. The conditions of trails are subject to change very rapidly due to weather and erosion. A trail which was obvious may disappear in the snow or under rising water, a false trail may lead in the wrong direction and bridges, natural and otherwise can wash out leading to trail reroutings. Sometimes landmarks which seemed so obvious at the outset become obscured as night descends, fog rolls in, or fatigue clouds judgment. For these reasons, always carry detailed maps of the area you are traveling through, perhaps several types. With an appropriate map and compass and the knowledge to use them comes the confidence to know where you are and how to get home.

Experienced hikers are always thinking in terms of contingencies. No matter how unlikely it seems, always plan as if you will become lost. How will anyone know where to look if you don't return? How will you stay warm if you are injured and must spend a night in the bush before help arrives? What if the weather forecast is wrong and there is heavy rain? All of these possibilities should suggest steps to be taken.

A headlamp keeps hands free if forced to travel after sunset and is a better choice than a flashlight. Remember that a bright light will cause the pupil of the eye to contract and reduce night vision. Delay putting on the flashlight and once on, avoid flashing it in the direction of anyone's face. It is a natural tendency to turn and face the person being spoken to. While wearing a headlamp this will cancel out the other person's night vision and it will take some time for their eyes to readjust.

Every once in a while a hiker will spend an unplanned night in the bush. If delayed by bad weather or injuries, the danger of hypothermia increases. Clear, cloudless nights mean that the heat will radiate away from the ground and temperatures will drop. The evaporation of sweat from the day's exertions will cool the body. At higher elevations the warm and pleasant morning at the base can become a freezing night. The day hiker should always consider the possibility that he will be spending the night outside and should take sufficient clothing for the coldest night anticipated whether or not intending to camp out. The longer the trip the greater the chance that the weather will change. In the mountains weather can change within an hour. It is prudent to take rain gear even if the weather seems fine at the trailhead and no rain is in the weather forecast. A heavy morning dew can make you just as wet as a downpour and you will need rain gear just as much.

Each year people perish in the bush after a snowfall. The danger is, of course, that the snow covers the trail that they are following. In alpine areas, feet are very destructive to the vegetation. It takes very few feet per year to create trails and flagging is not necessary. There is often little vegetation to attach flagging to and the harsh weather means the flagging does not stay up long. Trails disappear where they encounter bedrock and routes are marked by piles of rocks or cairns. A little snow will cover evidence of the trail and any cairns. A route which was obvious in the morning may have disappeared by afternoon beneath the snow. Your own tracks or those of others are not always dependable route markers. A hiker may turn at the end of the day and find that trail markings are gone and his own tracks are not easily visible. Fresh snow may have covered the tracks or they may have melted under a bright sun and no longer be visible.

The proficient use of map and compass cannot be learned by reading alone. Like driving a car, route finding requires a good deal of practice to achieve mastery. With mastery comes the freedom to go where one pleases on trail or off, to feel confident and at home in the bush and to always know one's general position and heading. Along the road to easy confidence few like to admit to being lost or turned around but it has happened to all of us more often than we care to admit.

The first and most difficult part of being lost is to stop and take stock, to still the emotions. Once the rational mind takes over, try to recall the last point you are certain of. How long ago were you confident of your position? What were the landmarks that allowed confidence of that position? Can you find that position again? How long would it take to get back to that position? From where you are now, can you see any landmarks? There is bound to be disagreement between members of the group — but many heads actually are better than one. The headstrong person certain of his own convictions should be forced to explain his reasoning to the other members of the group and obtain their concurrence. Being lost is a situation that affects everyone equally and demands a consensus decision. Traveling in the wrong direction will be worse than doing nothing and waiting for rescue. Staying put is a viable option. Take half an hour to rest, talk, and think things through.

You may decide to await rescue for a number of reasons. You admit you are lost, you are injured and cannot proceed, you are not lost but visibility is reduced: darkness has fallen, there is heavy snowfall or you are fogbound. You realize that if you proceed you may become lost. Now is the time to think in terms of the search efforts which will be mounted by the authorities to locate you and extract you from your predicament.

In some cases, you may be able to initiate the search through the use of a personal locator beacon or cell phones. If you have distress flares do not waste them. The flares will be more visible when it is dark. By then, people will know that you are missing and be more likely to sight your flare. If you fail to return, who will be the first to know? When are you expected? What did you tell people about your trip? If you are in an area frequented by hikers and skiers, the authorities will have established a procedure for mounting a search and rescue operation.

In Canada, air and ocean-based searches are the responsibility of the Canadian military. Local police are responsible for ground searches for hikers. For most of Canada, it is the RCMP who will initiate the search and call upon whatever search and rescue resources are available. In the United States the umbrella organization for search and rescue is NASAR (National Association for Search and Rescue of Chantilly, Virginia). The principle, however, remains the same: a lost person is a missing person and therefore the local police will be the agency contacted first.

The cardinal rule for bush travelers is to tell a reliable person

START: _____ _____ / _____
         Day of Week   Date   Month

INTENDED
RETURN: _____ _____ / _____
          Day of Week   Date   Month

PURPOSE OF TRIP:

☐ Day Hike   ☐ ½ Day Hike

☐ Overnight Hike   ☐ Climbing

☐ Fishing   ☐ Hunting

☐ Skiing   ☐ Snowmobiling

☐ Canoeing/Kayaking   ☐ Mushroom Picking

☐ Other: _____

THE TRIP:

General Area: _____

Specific Area: _____

Intended Route in (be specific): _____

Intended Route out (be specific): _____

Destination: _____

Local Landmarks: _____

Map Used: _____

Hunting and Fishing Regulations Management Unit:

Fresh Water Fishing Regulations Synopsis Unit:

TRANSPORTATION TO AND FROM
THE STARTING POINT:

Vehicle Licence No.: _____

Make/Model: _____ Colour: _____

Owner: _____

or **Dropped Off at Starting Point by:**

Name: _____ Phone: _____

To Be Picked Up at End Point by:

Name: _____ Phone: _____

Time: _____ Date: _____

Location: _____

Other rendezvous points used by the group: _____

EQUIPMENT/SUPPLIES TAKEN:

☐ Backpack   ☐ Water   ☐ Firestarter

☐ First Aid Kit   ☐ Flashlight   ☐ Whistle

☐ Avalanche Beacon (PIEPS)   ☐ Snowshoes

☐ Stove   ☐ Skis   ☐ Extra Clothing

☐ Sun Protection   ☐ Tent (colour): _____

☐ Food (days per person): _____

☐ Radio (type and frequency): _____

☐ Signalling Device: _____

☐ Personal Locator Beacon (PLB #): _____

☐ Cellular Phone No.: _____

☐ Firearms: _____

☐ RV, ATV, Boat (description): _____

Fig. 8.2: A detailed trip itinerary. Leave it with a friend or family member and let him know when you will contact him again.

where they are going and when they expect to return. People die in the bush each year before anyone knows they are missing. By the time a search is organized, hypothermia may have claimed another victim. When traveling in remote areas of northern Canada, hikers and canoeists file trip itineraries with the RCMP (see figure 8.2). Needless to say this creates the obligation to advise the police and the primary contact person promptly upon emerging from the bush. It also obligates one to follow the original trip plan. If the route or objective changes while on the trail, one will be in an area that potential searchers will not initially consider a viable search area. Should the decision to alter the trip

DESCRIPTION OF THIS TRIP'S MEMBERS: DETACH AND LEAVE THIS HALF WITH A FRIEND

	Person 1	Person 2	Person 3	Person 4
Last Name				
First Name				
Disability				
Age				
Height				
Weight				
Hair and Skin				
20/20 Vision?				
Family Doctor				
Hat Colour				
Coat Colour				
Shirt/Sweater				
Pant Colour				
Footwear Type				
Personal Preparedness				
Survival Training				
Outdoor Experience				
First Aid				
Avalanche Awareness				
Skier				
Snowshoer				
Other				

THE FOLLOWING WILL BE NOTIFIED IF I / WE CHANGE DESTINATION:

Name: _____ Address: _____

Home Phone: _____ Work Phone: _____

PLEASE NOTIFY THE POLICE IF I / WE DO NOT RETURN BY:

Date: _____ Time: _____

Signature: _____ Date: _____

Fig. 8.2: Page 2.

plan arise before leaving the trailhead, leave a note in the vehicle of the latest plan. The authorities will check the trailhead and a note left on the dashboard or on the seat will guide their efforts.

I often travel solo and have developed the habit of deliberately leaving tracks. A footprint is like a signature. Along the route are encountered "track traps." These are areas of unmarked snow or soft ground in which obvious and complete footprints can be left. Even an untrained tracker can find the tracks and ascertain direction. Do not assume, however, that search and rescue organizations have tracking capabilities — they probably won't. But an obvious track in an obvious place has a high probability of being seen. If returning by the same route, you can "sign off." This means putting another track in the track trap to show that you have passed that way on your return trip.

Having been notified by friends or family, the authorities will attempt to gain as much relevant information about the missing party as they can in order to establish a search strategy. How many hours or days was the trip to take? By the time the authorities are involved, how much time has elapsed? What was the destination and route? What kind of clothing and survival gear were carried? What are current weather conditions and is the gear appropriate? What is the general physical condition and are there any medical conditions which may have created an emergency? Are there any children or elderly involved? What is the group's familiarity with local terrain and conditions? The trip plan was designed by search and rescue authorities. It was prepared in order to make searches as rapid and effective as possible. It depends, however, on hikers having the foresight to write the information down and leave it with a responsible person.

All of these factors help the authorities to assess the seriousness of the situation and the urgency of their response. The information will help them determine the type of search to conduct. A search for seasoned and well-equipped hikers late from a one week hike will be handled differently than a search for ill-equipped novices overdue from a day hike.

Additional information will help them in their search. What kind of footwear and color and type of clothing was worn? If the type of footwear is known, the probable tread pattern will help to distinguish your tracks from those made by others. Were tents or flares carried? What color is your tent?

Urban centers are likely to have trained volunteer search and rescue (SAR) organizations which can respond quickly to emergencies in and around the urban center. These volunteers are aware that a cold night in the bush may be fatal for the ill-equipped. It is not unusual for SAR groups to mount rapid response searches immediately upon being called, even during the night. Night searches are conducted in the dark regardless of weather conditions along known trails. These rapid night searches will be followed by more comprehensive daytime searches both on and off the trail.

Experience has shown that these night-time searches are effective for a number of reasons. Darkness usually keeps the victim in one place and prevents the situation becoming worse. If the victim has only been missing for a few hours it can be assumed that he is on or near his intended route. The search area is confined during the night. The more hours of daylight, the further the subject may have traveled. Perhaps he has been seen at a certain location by others who may still be in the area and available to be interviewed. Day hikers typically are ignorant of the dangers of hypothermia and do not carry emergency clothing. As the subject succumbs to the effects of hypothermia, he will become unresponsive to the shouts and whistles of rescuers and will eventually slip into unconsciousness. Most troubling of all are hypothermia victims, often children, who have been known to hide from searchers or to try to escape from them. Large-scale searches depend on the responsiveness of the subject. If the victim is injured but otherwise alert, he can see and hear searchers at a distance. This makes the searchers' job easier. Over time a lost person may become uncommunicative and many more searchers are required to cover the same area.

---

1   Rawicz, *The Long Walk*

2   Syrotuck, *Analysis of Lost Person Behavior*

9.

FIRE

FIRE HAZARDS

Forest fires have a profound impact both on the forest industry and recreational users of the wilderness. Lightning causes 37% of wildfires, 25% are caused by industrial activity such as logging, and the remaining 38% by the public engaging in recreational or other pursuits. While foresters appreciate the importance and necessary role of some fire in the regeneration and renewal of forests, it is clear that many fires are caused by humans and are preventable. As campers who are careless with their food create rodent and bear problems and those who are careless with their toilets spread disease to others, hikers careless with fire may cause destruction days after their departure. A fire can smolder for many days before bursting into flames. While canoeing in a remote area, my daughter and I came upon a forest fire burning its way along the forest floor — a ground as opposed to a surface or crown fire. We spent half a day fighting the fire with an axe, shovel, and pails of water and never saw another human being or knew who started the fire.

Hikers are unlikely to be trapped by a forest fire, mainly because the smell of smoke carries a long way. From afar the columns of smoke can be white to black depending on the type of vegetation burning and its water content. Up close a raging forest fire roars like a freight train. If you feel threatened, stay calm and stay together. Never try to outrun a forest fire. The fire will move with the wind, usually moving more quickly uphill than down and favoring southern slopes where the vegetation is drier. As winds pick up the fire burns hotter and spreads faster. Evasive action means moving out of the path of the fire or immersing oneself in a lake or river. Caves or wells should be avoided since oxygen will be cut off. An area which has already burnt is a good choice as there will be scarce fuel left for the fire to burn. Immediately following a fire the trees left standing will often have damaged root systems and in a wind, falling snags (called widow-makers) become a hazard. This is one reason why authorities keep areas closed even after a forest fire.

Always check with the park or government agency which assesses fire hazard. The level of fire risk changes from day to day and is not always obvious to the casual hiker. It is a complex assessment. I have walked an urban forest parched dry from prolonged drought. The forest floor was well stocked with flammable material, the nights had been warm and free of dew, daytime temperatures high and skies clear. The trails of this urban forest were made from layers of wood chips now tinder dry. Ahead of me on the trail were smokers with cigarettes dangling carelessly from their fingers. Smokers must be extra vigilant if they are to enter the forest.

Even if a fire is legally allowed and any necessary permits obtained, consider if a fire is really necessary. Fires are an awkward way to cook food compared to stoves and bug spray is far more effective than fires at keeping bugs at bay. Will the group be spending the evening around the campfire or will the fire be soon forgotten? Once the fire is going, someone must stay near to watch it. It will take a long time to burn itself completely out and leave only ashes. Too many fires are left to burn themselves out leaving charred wood and black embers which will lie on the ground for years to come. Responsible campers will stop feeding the fire long before bedtime and give the fire lots of time to burn out. All the unburned ends and charred bits and pieces can be fed back into the hottest part of the fire. In this way, only ashes will be left behind. A layer of earth or a few pots of water are extra insurance to be sure the fire is out and cannot spring back again. In the months to come, the fire's ashes will gradually return to the soil under the influence of wind and rain: charred wood will not.

Fires can't be moved once they are started and should be sited carefully. In deference to the environment it is advisable and considerate to use an existing campfire site. Fire will sterilize the ground it is set on and the evidence can last for many years; archaeologists study campfires hundreds of years old. It is the antithesis of no-trace camping. When choosing a campfire location be aware of the wind. Will it blow sparks into dry branches or into tents or camping gear? If cooking over a fire in bear country, it should be located downwind and several hundred feet from the tents to keep food smells away.

Be sure that the fire is built on rock or earth. Take the trouble to clear away any dry vegetation or other flammable material. Use a spade or boot heel to dig down to soil and clear a large enough area, bigger than the fire will be. A solid base for the fire not only prevents forest fires but improves the chances of a successful fire. Rock or earth will reflect heat back into the fire enabling the heat to build up. The hotter the fire, the more self-sustaining it will be. Consider nearby trees, branches and underbrush. The drier the conditions, the stronger the wind, the greater will be the need to set back the fire from foliage. A fire lit next to a rock will reflect heat back and will also provide protection for the fire from the wind. A root or log will not do. A fire built against such wood may spread unseen below the wood or enter cracks. It may smolder there for days before flaring up. On snow the problem is keeping the fire from sinking. A bed must be made if no rocks are available: green logs, green branches or ideally a piece of sheet metal raised above the snow and resting on rocks.

If the forest floor catches a spark or becomes hot enough, the fire can smolder after the campfire is out, traveling along unseen before erupting into a forest fire days later. The forest fire mentioned earlier was probably of this type. The fire was burning its way along the forest floor in an area about the size of a baseball diamond. Trees and underbrush would burst into flame as the advancing embers reached them. If a strong wind had come up, the fire could not have been stopped. The flames would then have spread from tree to tree rather than traveling along the ground.

FIRE MAKING

Fire making is a skill that few have mastered. In a park campsite on a quiet summer evening with dry wood at hand, practically anyone can make a fire. But what if we desperately need a fire? Picture yourself away from dry firewood, cold and miserable, soaked to the skin and starting to shiver. The forest is dripping with rain, the wind is blowing and darkness is falling. The paradox is that the more we need a fire the more difficult it will be to make one. People often succumb to hypothermia not because they lack the means to start a fire, but because they lack the skill.

A campfire has four requirements:

a)   ignition
b)   tinder
c)   kindling
d)   fuel

All of these requirements should be on hand before the match is struck. Assemble tinder, kindling, and fuel so that you are not distracted from the process or worse yet, allow the fire to go out while you search for dry materials. The goal is to have a "one match" fire. When you leave the fire should be nothing but fine white ashes.

a) Ignition

Survival experts are full of suggestions for starting fires without matches: a broken piece of glass to use like a magnifying glass (one authority even suggests shaping a piece of ice into a magnifying glass), rubbing sticks together or making a bow and fire drill the way the Natives did, shorting out a battery to use the sparks, taking a rifle or shotgun shell apart to fire the powder into some tinder. Some of these techniques may work but unless you have practised a lot I wouldn't count on them. The Natives went to great lengths to avoid having their fires go out; those in the Mackenzie River Valley were known to carry their embers in earthen pots from place to place. When the first Europeans made contact with Inuit, the Inuit were very eager to get matches. Matches were highly valued and traditional techniques abandoned. They carefully split each match into two or four smaller matches just to avoid the difficulties of starting a fire with rock and flint. Clearly, if we city folk are going to get a fire going, we are going to need matches. Many hikers prefer a lighter because it can provide a longer-lasting flame. I recommend that these people also carry matches. They are a back-up in case the lighter fails. Matches are low tech and if used in conjunction with a short stubby candle the flame will have ample opportunity to light the tinder. Matches can get lost or left behind so carry extras in several places: with the stove, with food, and in your pack. If they can be kept dry — a film canister works very well — you probably don't need to buy special waterproof ones. Don't leave matches out in the open. Open the canister, use the match, and immediately put the rest away. That way the matches won't get dropped, rained on, stepped on, or lost.

b) Tinder

Tinder is the smallest, driest, most flammable material you have available. Historically, travelers have not trusted that they would always find tinder when they needed it. Tinder was gathered and carried from place to place in tinderboxes, pouches, or horns. Before matches were used, a steel knife was struck on a flint stone. The resulting sparks were directed at tinder and the spark nursed into a flame. A modern-day tinderbox can be a plastic bag with the discarded paper and cardboard food packaging kept in it. Lint from a clothes dryer or dry hair from a hairbrush will work, although burning hair doesn't smell very good. In a pinch you can use part of a map or some extra toilet paper. If using stove fuel for ignition, use extreme caution to ensure the flame doesn't travel back into the fuel container. If unsuccessful in getting the fire going, beware of pouring gas on top of embers. Once the fire has started to burn, it is too late to add fuel from the bottle. Put fuel on a stick and put the stick on the embers. Be careful that you have not spilled fuel on your fingers. Fingers with fuel on them can burn too. Set the fuel bottle well away from the fire before striking the match.

The short stubby candles used for heating fondue pots or for warming food are also good for starting fires. These candles are much cheaper than the colored ornamental type and are a good emergency backup when fire making gets tough. Because they are short and wide, they won't tip easily and are a long burning focus for the fire. Commercial firestarter can be purchased to use as tinder. Petroleum-based firestarters have a strong odor and should be doublebagged to prevent the odor contaminating other things.

Nature's tinder is almost always available. Resin or pitch exuded from tree trunks is highly flammable and if conditions have been dry, look for any small dry material: conifer needles, old bird nests, bark, grass, or leaves. After continuous wet weather when there is hardly any dry material around it is time-consuming, but still possible, to make a fire. Look for a branch or sapling about the same diameter as your thumb. Cut a section about four inches long as cleanly as possible. (A small saw gives a better cut than a knife.) Split the section longitudinally into four equal quarters. Looking down the grain, each piece will look in cross section like a quarter of a pie. The centre of the branch is the centre of the pie and the bark layer is the pie crust. Each piece will have a portion of the branch core exposed. This core will be dry even though the outside layers of the branch may be too wet for tinder. Rest one end of the stick on something solid and make shavings of the innermost portion of the stick, leaving them still attached to the main stick. This is called a fuzzstick.

c) Kindling

Burning tinder is a tenuous fire; it lacks heat, has no embers, won't light any but the driest and smallest material and is particularly sensitive to wind and rain. At some point something more substantial than tinder must be made to burn. Kindling is small dry wood, more substantial than tinder, but smaller

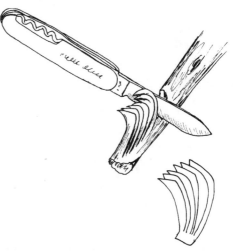

Fig. 9.1: Making a fuzzstick.

than fuel. Check to see that the wood is dry. It should not bend but break with a snap. With an axe or large knife split wood into small pieces. Start with short slivers of wood the diameter of wood matches, then introduce progressively larger pieces as the fire gets hotter. The easier the wood is to split the easier it is to make kindling. A piece of dry cedar is ideal, some hikers will carry a piece of cedar roofing shake just for kindling.

d) Fuel

When the fire generates enough heat to burn kindling the size of a finger, you are ready to add fuel. Fuel need not be completely dry because the fire will have enough heat to dry it before burning.

The fire is past the fussy stage. Scavenge fuel from dead branches and windfalls. It is not necessary to chop down trees. There is usually plenty of fuel lying on the forest floor or along watercourses. If other people have frequented the area, clean up the remains of their campfires by burning charred material they left behind. Clean up the campsite by burning the garbage, yours as well as what others have left; forgotten string, tissue, and packaging.

CAMPFIRE COOKERY

Cooking over an open fire can sometimes be a challenge. The most elementary technique is to balance the pot on a rock with one edge of the pot hanging over the fire. A more sophisticated technique is to locate two flat rocks and space them just far enough apart so that the pot will bridge the gap. Then try to coax the fire into the space between the rocks to heat the pot. Either way, the pot will likely heat unevenly. A small wire grate is an improvement. It can rest on rocks and be positioned over the fire. The pot is then resting on the grate rather than rocks and is less likely to tip. Cooking heat can be regulated more evenly because the pot can be moved from place to place on the grate.

Use pots with pail-like handles to enable lifting with a stick instead of burning bare fingers. This type of handle will also facilitate hanging the pot over the fire. Carry a piece of flexible wire for this purpose instead of string or rope which may burn or melt and allow the food to drop in the fire. Position a strong stick over the flames or fashion a tripod with three sticks. The base of the tripod goes outside the fire ring and the other ends are joined together over the fire with a wire. Suspend the pot above the fire. All these techniques, however, will result in a black-bottomed pot and the black soot will rub off on fingers and other gear. Keep the pot and grate in its own protective bag.

Fish can be cooked over a fire without a pot or frying pan. Clean the fish. Fillet it if it is large enough. Then skewer the fish on a green branch and roast it like a hot dog over the fire. I have fond memories of ice fishing in a stream and cooking and eating our catch in front of a fire on the bank.

BUGS, SIGNALS, AND DRYING OUT

Fires have other important uses for hikers besides cooking. A fire, and the resultant smoke, can be used as protection against biting insects. Although given a choice between applying bug dope or standing in the smoke from a fire most hikers will choose the former.

Lost hikers can often be located most easily with a fire. The smell of smoke carries a long distance in calm air and is highly visible, particularly from aircraft. Lost hikers are well advised to start a fire. It will aid in the search, provide warmth and comfort, and keep them in one place and focused while search activity is being carried out.

Care must be taken with most modern synthetic fabrics as they are more easily damaged by heat and sparks than traditional fabrics. Most hikers are too impatient. I have burnt holes in a few pairs of socks. Polypropylene and nylon will melt and congeal into hard lumps. These lumps will be most uncomfortable against the skin. If socks are destroyed by the fire you are in trouble unless you brought a spare pair. Polyester jackets which receive sparks dissolve, leaving holes in the material. Wool socks can also be damaged and burn but they tolerate heat better than synthetics. When drying clothing, check to see how hot the cloth surface is and keep tents and clothing well away from sparks.

Leather boots must not become too hot either. The leather can be damaged and the waterproofing applied to the boots will be lost. Then the boots will get wet again even faster. There is not much hope of re-waterproofing your boots until you get home and your boots have had a few days to dry completely. Touch the leather as it is drying. The leather surface can be warm but not hot. Drying clothes by the fire takes a long time. That's why it is best to take spare clothing. Don't rush it and be careful with your gear. You may start with wet gear and end up with damaged gear.

10.

FOOD

It is advisable to put the matter of food in perspective. Hikers starving in the bush are almost unheard of and there are many instances of adults surviving a month or more without food with no long-term effect. Indeed some health gurus advocate an occasional week-long fast in order to rid the body of toxins. After a few days, food ceases to be central in one's mind. If healthy and otherwise comfortable you can survive for a long while without food. The original bush dwellers, the aboriginal people, lived in a hunter gatherer society where seasonal food shortages were always a possibility. Food, over the short term, is not a matter of survival but of comfort and convenience. Water or fluids are a much more urgent consideration. When traveling in the bush, food becomes one of the high points of the day, the mind starts to think about supper long before camp is reached and almost anything tastes good in the outdoors!

Food is a pleasure but in the bush can be troublesome. Cooking without fridge, kitchen stove, oven, cupboards, or sink requires a disciplined approach. There are no convenience stores for treats or forgotten items. Meal preparation begins at home with the meal plan. The choice of food will depend on the length of the trip. A day trip requires practically no planning, a weekend trip a bit of thought, a week-long trip a lot of thought and for trips longer than a week, detailed and lengthy planning. Here are some criteria for food selection.

Is there any chance that the food will make a mess? Can the container break, rupture, split or tear? Glass containers should never go in the bush. If the glass breaks, how would the pieces be carried out? Hiking supply stores sell empty plastic food tubes which can be filled and squeezed like a tube of toothpaste. Be careful with the squishables or items wrapped in plastic bags or tin foil. Most dry food travels well as do canned goods. Cans themselves are not heavy, it is the water in the can which adds the weight. After using the can, remove the label and burn it, wash the can and flatten it between two rocks. Store used food containers with other garbage and make certain that it goes into a bear cache at night, away from the tents.

Weight is the obvious limiting factor for food. No hiker will want to carry more than a couple of cans. If water will be available along the trail, then there is little point in carrying food packed in liquid. Look for freeze-dried or dehydrated food items and read the weight on the package. Then look for the amount of water to be added to the contents — the higher the ratio of water to food, the more the food swells up with water, the less will be the weight in relation to the available food. Beware, however, of cooking times. If one food cooks in two minutes and the other is ready in ten minutes, the latter will take five times as much fuel. What is gained in lighter food is lost in the amount of fuel which must be carried. Check cooking times on the package and leave the foods which require a lot of cooking for those times when you will be cooking over a campfire rather than a stove.

Food spoilage is always a consideration when traveling far from proper refrigeration. Salmonella, botulism and other perils of improper food handling don't take a holiday and when the sun beats down on a pack, food spoilage is accelerated. Meats, even if smoked, will not have normal shelf life and the prospect of food poisoning along with vomiting and diarrhea is not a pleasant prospect away from proper toilet and laundry facilities. Cured meats are also liable to attract the attention of bears and other scavengers. Forgoing meat in favor of the available vegetarian options, at least for the duration of a trip is a wise choice. The nuts in trail mix will last without refrigeration and provide lots of protein.

Many hikers prefer to prepackage each meal. Each day's cereal or trail mix is premeasured and placed in its own double plastic bag. If there are other ingredients to add, such as powdered milk to dehydrated potatoes, measure the ingredients and put them in a bag at home. When mealtime comes, just measure the water into the pot and dump in the contents; one bag per meal with perhaps an extra day's rations. The next step would be to have each day's meals together in a larger plastic bag. If wanting to be highly organized, label each bag for the appropriate day of the trip. If food, such as cereal or flour, needs to be measured on the trail, carry a plastic measuring cup which can double as a drinking cup.

The entire food supply should then be contained in its own bag. All of this bagging is important to keep ingredients dry and help to avoid spillage and waste. It also controls the escape of food smells. Food which is contained in multiple plastic bags is far less likely to be detected by bears, mice, squirrels, or insects. This is the single most important step to take to avoid bear problems. Avoid spicy foods for the same reason. If all the food is in its own bag, there is a further barrier between food odors and clothing and other gear in the pack. Ideally a food bag should have attachments to mount it on the outside of the pack. In this way, there is no intermingling of food smells with gear. At night the food bag can be unstrapped, kept near at hand while preparing meals and then hauled by rope into a bear cache.

Empty food packaging will continue to give off food odors. Far better to finish the food and burn the packaging in the campfire. If there is no campfire, the packaging should be properly sealed in a plastic bag and stored with the food and not left about the campsite overnight. Pots, plates, and cutlery should be washed promptly after use and the dishwater disposed of well away from camp. Leftovers are a no-no when camping. Apart from the wasted effort of carrying food not eaten, there is the problem of disposal without creating animal problems. If camping at a popular campsite, rats and mice may frequent the area — a direct result of campers who have come before you leaving food about the campsite. Burying food is not always effective either; bears and other animals can smell the food and will dig it up. Burning or carrying it home is required. Disposing in swift-moving water is effective but not environmentally sound.

On one or two-day hikes one can have a more relaxed attitude to food weight. I like to carry fresh fruit like apples and pears which help to quench the thirst and keep for a few days even in a hot pack. A box of crackers goes in the pack, too. Crackers are light, contain a bit of salt, and are good anytime. The box keeps the crackers from being broken and the cardboard becomes a handy fire starter. As the crackers dwindle in number, rip off cardboard to make the box smaller and use to start fires.

Hot breakfast cereal is light when dry and bulks up when water is added. In the case of cornmeal, one cup of dry cornmeal bulks up dramatically with four cups of water. Cream of Wheat bulks up one cup of cereal to three and a half cups of water. Smaller appetites can use prepackaged envelopes of cereal which are ready almost instantly. Add boiling water, stir and eat. Cornmeal requires very little fuel to cook. Bring the water to a boil, stir in the cornmeal with raisins for sweetener then remove from the stove. The cornmeal is ready long before it is cool enough to eat. Cornmeal's drawback is that it hardens like cement on pots and cutlery if allowed to dry. Carry a scouring pad and wash the pot and spoon soon after eating. Several cups of tea after the cereal and one is fully hydrated. If traveling in an area of questionable water, boil some extra water for your water bottle.

Lunch is eaten on the go. No one wants the trouble of cooking during the day. Trail mix is everyone's favorite. Any combination of dried fruit, nuts, and chocolate will do. Throw in a granola bar for a snack and you've got lots of calories to keep you going during the exertions of the day. The crackers are bulky but they are a light, quick food. On short hikes, sandwiches take unusual shapes when they are squished in a pack. Try pita bread sandwiches as they are more durable.

The stove comes out again for supper to cook a package of dehydrated pasta or rice dinner. Measure the amount of water required as stated on the package and possibly add some dehydrated vegetables (this will take a bit of extra water). The result is a one pot meal. If you hate dishes and are cooking for one — all that is needed is a spoon to eat out of the pot. Bring a dish with a high rim around the edge. Sitting on the ground with a hot plate balanced on your knee, it can sometimes be a little tricky to keep the food on the plate. A metal pie plate or stainless steel camping plate will work well. Use a mug with a handle so that fingers don't get burned.

11.

WATER

FLUID BALANCE

One can survive without food for many weeks. Survival without water, however, is measured in days. Eating requires water — food cannot be digested without fluid. If there is a shortage of water, eating will only increase dehydration. It is, therefore, advisable to eat sparingly if there is no water. Fluid is lost not only through perspiration but in the very act of breathing. Moist air from the lungs is exchanged for drier air from the environment. Hiking at higher elevation will increase the rate of fluid loss from breathing. Relative humidity decreases with elevation. At 13,120 ft (4,000 m)[1], relative humidity will have decreased by 75%. The amount of water lost through the skin increases at higher elevations where solar radiation is greater; sunburn will accelerate fluid loss through the skin. The exertions of a hike will cause the need for fluid replenishment to skyrocket. A 6 mile (10 km) fun run is over in less than an hour but race organizers know that they must provide water to the runners at the midpoint. Drink more fluid than the body needs and you will have to make an extra bathroom stop. Drink less fluid than the body needs and you may have a medical emergency. Inadequate fluid balance is associated with a variety of medical problems: heat cramps, heat exhaustion, and heat prostration in the summer and frostbite and hypothermia in the winter. The body's need for water may develop before a person feels thirsty. An adult hiker fully exerting herself on a hot summer day will require up to 1 gallon (4 L) of water. This exceeds the amount that a backpacker can reasonably carry.

Campsites are usually chosen for their proximity to a potable water source. When on the trail where future water sources are uncertain, I discipline myself to drink four cups of tea before leaving camp. If there is any question about the purity of the water, you will be able to boil it while you have the stove out and are preparing breakfast. Put extra water in the water bottle to drink during the day along the trail. Bring the water to a rolling boil and boil the water for a full minute. Four cups is a lot to drink but it means that one is fully hydrated and fine for a good part of the day regardless of whether suitable water is available along the trail. At each water source along the way, make it a rule to have a cup of water whether thirsty or not. Under exertion, the feeling of being thirsty is frequently delayed and it is better to drink when there is water available than to become dehydrated when there is none.

The easiest way to determine the body's hydration level is to observe the color of the urine. If urine is copious and colorless, you are fully hydrated. As dehydration sets in, urine flow decreases and begins to darken and you may begin to feel light-headed or dizzy. If urine becomes very dark or you are sweating heavily and can't remember when you last urinated, you are dehydrated regardless of whether you feel thirsty or not.

Heat cramps are severe muscular contractions: usually in the legs or abdomen. Treatment includes resting to let the body cool, drinking fluids and gently stretching or massaging the affected muscles.

More serious than heat cramps is heat exhaustion. The symptoms of heat exhaustion are more generalized, including dizziness, nausea, and headache. This is definitely time to stop until the person affected has recovered. Let him rest in a cool place and provide him with water to drink. Failure to stop and reverse heat exhaustion can lead to the potentially fatal condition of heat stroke.

Symptoms of heat stroke include high temperature, irrational behavior, rapid shallow breathing and eventually loss of consciousness. Heat stroke is a medical emergency. First aid is similar to that for heat exhaustion. The affected person should rest in a cool place. Assist the process by cooling the body by fanning or the application of wet cloths. If conscious, the person should be given cold water to drink.

Fluid balance is essential for proper temperature regulation during the heat of summer and is also important during the winter months. Insufficient fluids are a contributing cause of both frostbite and hypothermia. Loss of fluid volume impacts the body's ability to circulate warm blood. Obtaining sufficient water is obviously more complicated in winter when the streams are frozen and the ground covered with snow. Snow is not a substitute for water and one should not try to drink by eating snow. If you are traveling in winter further than your water supply, bring a stove with extra fuel to make water. To attempt to eat snow instead of drinking water is to begin a loosing battle with hypothermia. You will cool the body and produce diarrhea or other digestive upset long before fluid needs have been met. Try to find water, even if this means breaking through a layer of ice to get at the water beneath. If only snow is available choose wet snow if possible and avoid using ice. Wet snow will melt more quickly and with less fuel consumption. Put the snow in a pot over your stove for melting. Add a little water if you have some left. Water in the bottom of the pot will allow the steam to rise into the snow above and hasten melting. If water cannot be found and snow cannot be melted for water the options are limited. If the sun is sufficiently strong you may be able to put snow inside a plastic bag and let the heat of the sun melt the snow. If there are drips from melting snow prop a cup under the drip and wait for the cup to fill.

GIARDIA AND CRYPTOSPORIDIUM

The Giardia parasite causes giardiasis, an infection commonly referred to as beaver fever. The Cryptosporidium parasite causes cryptosporidiosis. Both parasites are spread from the feces of one animal to the mouth and, therefore, body of another animal. The host animal can be a human, a beaver, or any one of a long list of wild or domestic animals. A person may harbor the parasite and exhibit no symptoms while still infecting others. The disease is spread primarily through contaminated surface water although it can also be transmitted through contaminated food. Direct person to person transmission arises through improper personal hygiene. With the absence of sanitary toilet practices a person who is a parasitic host can transfer the parasitic cyst, or oocyst, when handling food. The parasite is ingested and then grows and develops inside the new host. In the backcountry, food preparation is often shared and hygiene standards are low. The potential for spreading disease increases.

Unfortunately, backpackers may have brought Giardia and Cryptosporidium to wilderness areas where they were previously unknown. Improper toilet practices have meant that parasites and other contaminants have been washed into lakes and rivers. The parasite cysts can survive outside an animal host for long periods of time. Infected water may be cold, clear and inviting to drink. These waters may be either standing or flowing and because freezing may not kill the cysts, even melted ice may contain harmful parasites. When water containing the cysts is drunk by animal or man, the parasite develops in the new host and is carried to new areas. Humans are the most mobile host and are, therefore, the prime culprits in the spread of diseases to previously pristine areas. Once the parasite has been brought to a new area it will enter the resident animal populations which will cycle the disease through their own population thus providing a reservoir of parasites and a continuation of the disease. The finger is often pointed at the beaver and gives giardiasis the common name of beaver fever.

Symptoms of giardiasis can begin several days or even weeks after ingestion. Typically, the hiker will develop symptoms at home, after the trip has been completed. The disease is not fatal. Symptoms include: diarrhea, nausea, bloating and cramps. Diagnosis is by microscopic examination of the stool for the parasite cysts. Symptoms last one to three weeks although they can become chronic or recurring. The Cryptosporidium parasite is spread in the same way as Giardia and causes diarrhea and cramps which usually last for two weeks. More effective treatment is available for giardiasis than for cryptosporidiosis. Fecal contamination of water sources can also spread hepatitis A, salmonella, and typhoid fever.

NOWHERE TO FLUSH

Every wilderness traveler has a duty to those who come after them to be responsible with their toilet practices. Feces must be disposed of so that runoff does not contaminate surface water. Toilets must be well away from surface water, trails and camping areas.

Increasing numbers of wilderness users with fewer areas of wilderness to travel in have created a crisis. Canoeists traveling along popular routes are more frequently being required to bring toilets with them in their canoes. The sewage is carried from campsite to campsite until finally disposed of at the conclusion of the trip. It is only part of the solution to the problem of too many people. Already, pipe-like devices are available for hikers to store their feces while on the trail. The feces is wrapped and fitted into the tube. The longer the hiking trip the longer the tube.

Toilet paper has its own subset of problems. It takes far longer to dissolve and disappear than feces. Too many lookouts and campsites are surrounded by accumulations of toilet paper left lying about in various stages of decomposition. The toilet paper should be buried or burned. If this is impossible the toilet paper should be kept in a plastic bag and disposed of at home. Menstrual products should be disposed of in the same way with the added proviso that the blood may be of interest to bears and other animals who will dig up improperly disposed material.

Excrement should be buried. Since the top layer of soil is most biologically active this is the place where decomposition will occur most quickly. In most soils, a depth of 4 to 6 in (10 to 15 cm) is recommended. A small spade is ideal, although the heel of a hiking boot in soft soil will be sufficient to create a small trench. If there is a group traveling in a popular area, it is incumbent on someone to carry a spade. Dig the trench sufficiently large with the soil deposited to the side. After each use some of the soil can be sprinkled over the feces. When camp is struck, the last duty will be to cover over the latrine and tamp down the earth. The latrine should be located so that rain water or spring floodwaters will not wash over it. The latrine should be at least 300 ft (100 m) from streams, lakes, or other surface water. Do not use the dry channel of a stream bed or a gully which will fill up with rainwater after the summer dry period or a rocky surface where rains can wash the feces away. The latrine must remain in place long enough for decomposition to take place.

High elevation hiking is high impact hiking. The damage done to plant life is quite obvious. Human feet easily kill vegetation and produce rutted trails in the delicate vegetation. At high elevation the ground is frozen and covered with snow for most of the year. The climate is harsh and the growing season short. Biological activity is minimal. Food scraps left behind by hikers will not rot away as they would at lower elevations and neither will feces. The contamination will be long lasting. Try to keep alpine areas pristine; they are too delicate to tolerate human activity.

The smear technique is recommended to those traveling in the mountains above treeline or in other areas where biologically active soil is absent. After defecating, a stone is used to spread the feces on a rock surface. The rock outcropping should be exposed to the sun so that the sunlight will act to kill and neutralize germs. The smearing ensures that the layer of feces is thin and the process rapid. At higher elevation the sunlight will be more intense. Toilet paper is burned or packed out.

TOILET TECHNIQUE

Because of the problems associated with sanitation and sewage disposal, and because bathroom behavior is often the last thing on a hiker's mind during the planning stages of a trip, a case can be made for an in-depth discussion of backwoods toilet technique, To insure comfort on the trail one of the most important items to pack is toilet paper. Keep fresh toilet paper in a mug or other container that is sure to be remembered. Observe how much toilet paper you use. Everyone should bring their own supply with a little extra for reserve, remember that bad food or water will create extraordinary demands on the amount of toilet paper required. Save partially used rolls from home as two or more small rolls, doublebagged and packed in separate places are better than one big roll. If one roll gets wet or is left behind there will be a spare. Although, if one is caught without toilet paper, remember that a good portion of humanity does not use the stuff. It is possible to use leaves, moss, extremely fine sand or water to wash yourself — away from surface water. Exercise caution in using grass in place of toilet paper; broad green grass can cut like a knife, especially in sensitive places!

If affected by poor balance or leg cramps, it is best to get the toilet paper ready before squatting. Lower the pants below the knees but above the ankles. Up too high and the cloth will bunch up behind the knees and cause discomfort. Too low and the cloth will be in harm's way. Crouch down. Then pull the pants up and away by the crotch. Hold them up. Do not try to balance on your toes but keep the feet flat, this will angle your backside down. If more height is needed be careful what you stand on; it must be stable. Squat on a flat rock or log. If this is a group latrine, you will likely have a spade to dig deep enough so that an extra height will not be necessary.

In the winter it may be difficult to dig a latrine. The ground may be covered in snow or frozen. Try to get down to ground level and chip and break up the sod. The alternative is to bag it and carry it out.

Fig. 11.1: Small children may need help going to the bathroom.

Small children will require help. Have the child drop their pants to their ankles. Next stand behind the child and have them bend at the knees while you grab them under the thighs. Hold them over the hole and have them straighten their legs. They can then fire away. After they are done lower them to one side of the hole.

In the book, *How to Shit in the Woods* (Ten Speed Press, 1994), Kathleen Meyer describes the unique problem women have in urinating when no latrine is available. The usual squatting technique results in urine splattering back onto the legs and clothing. She recommends that women urinate in a posture similar to the one suggested above for small children, using two rocks, logs or other low surfaces which are adjacent to each other. Lower the pants to the ankles. Perch on the edge of one surface. Prop the feet up on the second surface. This technique may be more comfortable for women and avoids urine splatter.

WATER PURIFICATION

City dwellers accustomed to water being fluoridated, chlorinated and filtered feel a natural reluctance when faced with free-flowing water. We have discussed the potential dangers of drinking from contaminated water. Those dangers are real and becoming greater. At the same time, each hiker must evaluate the level of danger in their area and the precautions they intend to take. Park wardens will generally recommend complete treatment of all water at all times. Always be aware of what lies upstream from where you intend to draw water. Are there buildings, cabins, livestock, or other campers upstream? Has the water just melted off a glacier or flowed a hundred miles? Is it surface water draining from a field or water percolating through a forest hillside ? Is it cold or warm, clear or cloudy, still or flowing? If in a campsite frequented by other campers, where have these people been washing and going to the bathroom? When camped, the rule is to wash downstream and get drinking water upstream. The further the better. If near a river, look for small feeder streams for water. If at a lake, take water from where it flows into the lake rather than the water flowing out.

Boiling is the method of choice for making sure water is safe. If cooking food, boil some extra water for the water bottle. The higher the elevation, the lower the boiling temperature of water and the longer the water should be boiled. At 19,000 ft (5,800 m), boiling times should be five times as long as at sea level. Recommended boiling time varies according to what kind of organism you are trying to kill. Giardia cysts are killed even before the boiling point has been reached. Bacteria and viruses are less hardy. A recommendation of the Outdoor Recreation Council of British Columbia is to start with the best water available, then boil it for at least one minute.

Iodine, chlorine bleach, and water purification tablets are all chemical methods of water purification and will leave an aftertaste in the water. Cryptosporidium will not be killed by chlorine and iodine may be a bad choice for those with a thyroid problem, children, or pregnant women. All chemicals must be in contact with the water for a period of time to be effective and if the water is cloudy or cold, either more time or chemicals will be required. For water purification tablets, follow the manufacturer's instructions. If the water is clear add 4 drops of tincture of iodine to 4 cups (1 L) of water and let stand for one hour. If the water is murky add 8 drops. Household bleach (containing chlorine) can be used to disinfect water in the proportion of 4 drops of bleach to one imperial gallon or 1 drop of bleach per liter of water. Stir and let stand 30 minutes (a recommendation of the British Columbia Ministry of Health).

Water filters are a more expensive alternative but provide an immediate source of potable water without the delay involved in boiling or chemical treatments. To be effective, the manufacturer's instructions for filter cleaning and filter replacement must be followed. Weight and space are the main deciding factors, but there is no shortage of models to choose from. Check at a local outdoor store.

---

1   Maniguet, *Survival: How to Prevail in Hostile Environments*

12.

BEARS

CHANGING PERSPECTIVES

Expert opinion on bears and bear behavior has undergone a great deal of change over the last several decades and is prone to uncertainty and debate. Had I written this chapter ten or twenty years ago, the perspective would have been very different, particularly pertaining to black bears, which were considered relatively harmless. During the 1930s, public bear feedings were held in Yellowstone Park for the entertainment of visitors. In the 1960s, tourists handfed bears along park roadways. No doubt this relaxed attitude to bears and bear management gave rise to Yogi Bear, the impish but harmless cartoon bear who steals food from the park warden.

It then became generally accepted that bears can and do pose a threat to humans, although this was tempered with the belief that maulings were not normal bear behavior and people tended to blame the victim. According to this view, bears in a state of nature will not harm humans but, if they do, it is the humans who have caused the bear to attack. Research is now available which casts doubt on these beliefs and indicates that bear behavior is somewhat more complex. We know that in the vast majority of cases, bears seek to avoid contact with humans. This mutual avoidance strategy works for most bears, most of the time.

In the past, bears were an important food source for aboriginal peoples. In the fall, bear meat was prized for the amount of fat which it contained. There was no confusion as to who was the prey and who was the predator. Until recently in rural areas, a nuisance bear could expect a blast of buckshot to send it on its way. Such a bear learned to fear and avoid humans. This was primitive but effective bear management. The hunting pressure on bears has now eased. Increasingly bears have learned two lessons: they have nothing to fear from humans, and where there are humans, there is food. Many are completely protected because they live within park boundaries. Anecdotal evidence shows that more bears are being encountered now than in the last ten or twenty years and the bears are showing less fear of humans.

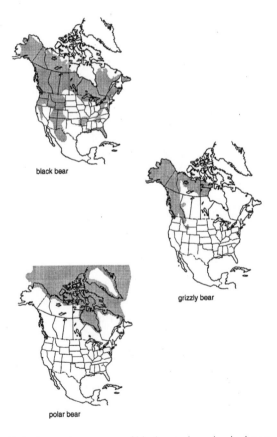

Fig. 12.1: Approximate range of black, grizzly and polar bears.

Designated campsites within parks have meant interesting food smells and occasional food for the bears. Not surprisingly, encounters between bears and campers increase with increased human intrusion. Park officials are torn between their desire to safeguard the bears and safeguard the people. Be aware of bear warning signs or park area closures. The park rangers have detailed local knowledge and their decision to close portions of the park due to bear hazard should be respected. These closures are for the protection and safety of the public.

A great deal of nuisance activity is tolerated and bears which become used to people are often simply relocated. There is now evidence that the relocated bear will return to its previous area or become a nuisance in its new location. We may be cultivating increased numbers of bears who not only have no fear of humans but associate humans with food. Such bears are said to have become "habituated" to humans. They are food-conditioned bears and will approach people for food and can be unpredictable and dangerous. In some cases it is believed that this food conditioning can reach a point where bears not only associate people with food but associate people as food. These bear attacks are classified as predatory and are often preceded by stalking type behavior.

BEAR BASICS

There are three major classifications of bears in North America: black bears, grizzlies, and polar bears. What type of bear are you likely to encounter?

Black Bear

Black bears are common throughout North America. They are smaller and more numerous than grizzlies. They are found over a wider range. This is the most common subject of a bear encounter. Black bears seem to accept living close to human settlement and will scavenge for human food in garbage dumps, orchards, or campsites.

The grizzly bear once roamed the western half of the continent, but is now extinct in much of its former range.

Color is not a reliable guide to determining species. Grizzlies range from cream to brown or black. Black bears are often black but can be brown, bluish

Grizzly Bear

or white. The adult grizzly is usually larger than the black bear and has a characteristic hump on its shoulder. The hump is a mass of muscle which the grizzly has developed for digging. It can dig in the earth for ground squirrels or rip apart rotten logs in its search for insects. This hump is absent in black bears. The grizzly has much longer claws — finger length, which are not good for climbing trees, but excellent for digging. The mark of these long claws help to distinguish a grizzly from a black bear track. The grizzly has a flat, disk shaped face.

In the spring, bears eat roots, new shoots, and mammals. When the winter snow melts, they will be attracted to the early growth on south facing slopes. When the berries form, bears feed extensively in berry patches and on grasses. During the fall, they continue to prepare for the coming winter and hibernation. They eat berries, roots, and mammals. Coastal bears will feed on spawning salmon and can be expected anywhere along such streams. As bears are nothing if not opportunistic, carrion is a favored food. When not actively feeding, bears will rest and remain near their food source.

The polar bear is the largest and most dangerous of the bears. They exhibit little fear of man and are known to hunt humans for food. They are the world's largest carnivore, weighing up to 1,500 pounds (700 kilograms). They are sometimes called sea bears, or ice bears because of their close assoc-

Polar Bear

iation with the arctic marine environment. They prey on seals and are excellent swimmers. During part of the year they leave the ice and range inland some distance from the ocean.

Bears are not food for any other animal and are at the top of the food chain, although they will attack and kill one another. Male bears will attack a female in order to eat their cubs. This probably accounts, in part, for the strong instinct sows exhibit defending their cubs. The continuation of the species requires it. Bears will fight each other over carrion. A hiker coming upon a sow bear with cubs or a bear protecting carrion is in danger.

AGGRESSIVE/DEFENSIVE BEHAVIORS

Kelly Mortensen is a man who knows the bush: professional guide, climbing instructor, and consultant to the film industry. In 1983, Kelly had just finished another day of teaching outdoor skills to high school students. Jogging ahead of the students along the trail, Kelly was only minutes from camp when he met the bears. Coming up a gully and around a sharp bend in the trail, Kelly could have reached down and touched the young cub with his left hand. In the same second that he saw the second cub to his right he heard the crashing in the bush. Kelly did not waste time turning to look. He knew he was going to be attacked by a mother bear. Running back along the trail, Kelly made it 30 feet (10 m) up a tree before the mother bear got to the base of the tree, and began to climb.

When the bear reached him, Kelly screamed at the bear. The bear bit down on the toe of Kelly's thick mountaineering boot. Kelly kicked the bear in the face with his free boot and the bear lost its grip on the tree. The bear's teeth slid over the toe and bit into the welt of the boot as it started to fall. Kelly was pulled by the boot. He started to fall and the bear released its grip. Hugging the tree as he slid down the trunk, the stubby branches gouged his face and chest. Then Kelly started back up the tree a second time with the bear in pursuit.

As the bear drew near, Kelly held the tree with his arms and kicked down on the bear's head with both feet. Both bear and Kelly fell down the tree a second time. Kelly made it up the tree a final time and again, waited for the bear. Blood was smeared across his face and fell down onto his shirt. Kelly knew he was probably going to die. Time seemed to stretch out as he braced himself to fight for his life. He would not die easily. He intended to gouge the bear's eyes if he could. Kelly drew his legs up and crouched in the tree. He was ready. The bear came within striking distance of Kelly. Bear and man stared at each other and Kelly looked the bear full in the face and saw the fire in its eyes. In a calm, controlled voice Kelly then said to the bear, "I am not going to hurt your cubs." Kelly says that at that moment the fire suddenly left the bear's eyes. The bear broke off the attack and backed down the tree. It charged its two cubs scattering them into the bush, then turned and charged the base of Kelly's tree three or four times. The bear needn't have worried. Kelly wasn't about to climb down. The bear then ambled away after its cubs.

Reconstructing the events later, Kelly says it was just bad luck. By running down the gully, the noise Kelly made was absorbed into the bank. The sudden turn in the trail meant the bears could not see him until he was upon them. The wind was in Kelly's face so the bears could not smell him. The sow bear had no way to know he was coming and no time to move her cubs away. Bears are opportunists; they go where there is easy food. Perhaps that is why they were so near camp. Adrenaline mixed with climbing skill got Kelly up the tree three times.

Black bears and young grizzlies climb trees. Mature grizzlies don't. There is an exception to this: the tree with conveniently placed limbs. A large grizzly can climb ladder-like rather than using his claws on the tree trunk. Being able to tell an adult grizzly from a black bear is more difficult than most people realize, but it is an important distinction.

STALKING AND PREDATORY BEHAVIORS

In 1995 Bart de Haas was 430 miles (700 km) into his solo hike across the far northern wilderness of British Columbia. Something made him look backwards. Following him along the trail was a young grizzly bear. When Bart sped up, the bear sped up. When Bart moved off the trail, the bear moved off the trail. Was this bear hungry or just curious? Bart unstrapped his rifle, chambered a shell and fired over the bear's head. It was not startled but did move away. That evening, looking up through the flap of the tent, he was surprised to see the same bear again. It was staring at him. Loading another shell, Bart fired over the bear's head. This time it did not move away. In fact, it didn't react at all to the rifle shot. With darkness falling, Bart had had enough. He was angry. Summoning a lungful of air, he shouted loudly. The shout did what the rifle did not. The bear dashed away and was not seen again.

In bear encounters it is the particular circumstances and the intent of the bear which is important. The bear which attacked Kelly Mortensen was acting defensively. Kelly got far too close to the cubs and the mother bear acted predictably. The bear continued to act aggressively until she was sure that the threat to her cubs was gone. The Bart de Haas story is equivocal. Was this just a young bear which had never seen a human before? Bears are known to be inquisitive, but this one seemed unusually persistent. Its behavior was more like a predator stalking prey. Was this bear stalking as a prelude to an attack?

The final category of bear encounter is the most troubling. The bear, for whatever reason, wants to kill you. The noises you make in the bush may attract it rather than cause it to flee. This is a predatory rather than a defensive response. The bear may see people as food. Many bears who have acted in this way have later been killed and found to have medical problems which precluded them from gathering sufficient food.

Playing dead is clearly the wrong strategy. If you are being stalked, you are being sized up. The bear is evaluating its chances of "taking you." If you run, the bear will know that you are easy prey and a bear can run much faster. If it is a black bear, it can climb trees, but a mature grizzly won't. You are in a fight for your life. There are no guarantees. Some people have escaped injury by taking off their packs, setting their packs down, and backing away as the bear advances. Sometimes the bear will stop to examine the pack. It may be satisfied with the pack particularly if it contains food. But an even more dangerous bear has been created. By stalking a human it has obtained food. Advise the authorities and hope that they will destroy the bear.

BEAR ENCOUNTERS

Humans rely primarily on their vision and, to a lesser extent, sound. Bears rely on their sense of smell, which is highly developed, together with their hearing. Their eyesight is less well developed than our own. If the wind is not blowing from you to the bear, the bear will not smell you. If the wind is rustling leaves or there is river noise, it cannot hear you coming. If it cannot smell you or hear you it can only depend on its least developed sense — sight. In this circumstance a close encounter with a bear becomes a possibility.

If you see a bear before it sees you, it is best to leave the area. Wait for the bear to look away and then slowly and carefully withdraw. If the bear has seen you, identify yourself as human, usually by talking to it. Let it evaluate the situation. You are not another bear who has come to attack it nor are you food. Be slow and deliberate in all actions — do not run. The bear may stand on its hind legs and look in your direction swaying from side to side. It is trying to see and smell you better. Move away slowly. If you move upwind from the bear, it will be able to smell you. This is not the time to act aggressively or to move towards the bear. Unless you are a bear expert, you will not know if the bear considers you to have invaded its space. Being too close depends on many factors. If you are too close the bear may already feel threatened. Moving towards the bear increases the risk of a defensive attack.

There may be occasions when a bear is coming towards you but is unaware of your presence. This is also a time to move out of the way, to avoid contact, and if necessary identify yourself as human. Show yourself and talk to the bear. Do not act aggressively, and do not run.

There are circumstances when the bear will choose not to move away. It may be protecting cubs or a food source. You may have blundered into a situation which will make it feel threatened. It may engage in threat display signals. This will include puffing, ears back, stomping or bluff charges. This behavior is intended to scare you and no doubt it will. The bear may charge. If this is a defensive action, it will usually charge without making contact. To avoid a charge show the bear that you are dangerous and attempt to make yourself as large as possible by raising your arms above your head and moving them slowly back and forth. Get up high. Stand on a log or rock. Yell. Jump up and down. The bear may repeatedly charge stopping just short or veering away at the last moment. You are trying to convince it not to fight you. Withdraw while facing it but do not run.

Sometimes the bear will make contact even though it is acting in defense. If you feel that it will make contact but its intention is defensive rather than predatory, then protect yourself as best you can. Adopt the fetal position. Curl up, protect your face and stomach. Do not struggle and do not scream. Interlace fingers clasping your hands together behind your neck. Assume that the bear will not harm you after it has determined that you are not a threat.

Fig. 12.2: Adopting the
fetal position with fingers
interlocked behind the
neck during an
aggressive/defensive
bear attack.

BEAR AVOIDANCE

Knowing how to avoid an encounter with a bear is important information. People who travel in groups are unlikely to encounter bears (or any other wildlife for that matter). Two people look more vulnerable to a bear than three; a lone person more vulnerable than two; a child or a person lying on the ground most vulnerable of all. This makes sleeping in a tent safer than sleeping under the stars. The more people, the less the chance of a bear encounter. With more people there is more noise, more human odor, and more motion to alert the bears to your presence. John Clarke is a Vancouver mountaineer who has spent a good part of his life traveling through the Coast Mountains of British Columbia. He carries an ice axe with him and bangs it on rocks when he encounters a bear. He claims that the unnatural pinging sound of steel against rock scares the bears away, although below the treeline, rocks may not always be handy and an ice axe banged against a tree sounds more familiar to a bear and does not work as well to discourage them. Hunters and people who hope to encounter wildlife travel solo. But if bear avoidance is a primary goal, travel in groups.

Some people who travel solo or in small groups in bear country attach bells to packs. This may be distracting and annoying, but if it gives peace of mind, and discourages bear encounters, it will be worth the minimal irritation. Remember that the sound these bells make is not loud and can be masked by wind and river sounds. Always make noise when passing through prime bear feeding areas. Avalanche chutes, logged off areas and old burns often have prime berry patches. The vegetation is low but dense and can easily hide a feeding bear. In berry patches, vocalize. Use whistles with caution. A grizzly will be attracted to the high pitched squeak of a marmot. No bear will mistake a human voice for a marmot's. It is definitely out of place in the bush. Carrion and fish spawning streams are natural attractions for bears. As earlier noted, bears will defend food sources, if you smell carrion in the bush, it is no time to go investigating unless you are armed. If you see birds circling a particular spot, it may be carrion.

Dogs can act as a potential early warning system as their senses are more acute. They will warn you of bears, although in parks dogs may be banned due to the danger they pose to wildlife. Even outside parks, an unleashed dog is of dubious value. Chances are that if the dog finds the bear, it will enrage it and a frightened dog is likely to run straight towards its owner. An unleashed and untrained dog can increase the likelihood of a bear encounter.

Know when you are in a bear area. Recognize bear sign. Bear scat is hard to miss and cannot be confused with anything else. It can be up to a foot across and usually black with a consistency between cow and horse droppings. Occasionally you will see a pile of half-digested food. Bears are real gluttons during the summer months as they try to take on enough fat to last them through the coming winter. If they overeat they will regurgitate the excess. They feed on insects, ripping apart old logs and turning over rocks in the search for food. Rotten logs are often seen partially broken apart and strewn about. Bears also mark trees with their claws. Watch for these markings and examine them. Can you see all five claws on each paw? How big would the bear be? Sometimes the claw marks can be seen going for a long way up the tree: a sign of a bear climbing a tree.

CAMPING CONCERNS

When selecting a campsite, be conscious of bear sign in the area. Are you camping in an area frequented by bears? Are there berries or other attractants nearby? Is this a campsite where others have camped? If the campers before you were careless with their food, the bears may be back. They have remarkable memories. You may pay the price for someone else's carelessness. I am meticulous in my handling of food; I take no chances. In the bush I sleep well knowing that I have taken all precautions. I expect bears to be afraid of me. I expect them to avoid my campsite, particularly if I have had a fire going. There is no smell of food, so they have no reason to come near. Car campers are not no-trace campers. They are high impact campers likely to leave food and rubbish about. There is no safety in numbers from food conditioned bears. I am safer by myself in the wilderness than camped cheek by jowl with neighbors in bear country.

Safe food practices begin with the choice of food. Grease is particularly attractive to bears. Burn excess grease and take care with greasy dishwater. Barbecued meats, chili and spices are fine at home. Spicy food does not belong in bear country.

A hiking partner and I had been climbing through an old logged off valley and into mature timber. We stopped on the mountainside beneath the upturned roots of a tree. We could look down the slope and to both sides but the roots blocked our view up the slope. Nothing above us on the slope could see us either. After we had been sitting quietly for ten minutes, we heard pounding on the slope above us. It was a terrible noise and was coming towards us down the slope somewhere behind the roots. A bear was racing full speed down the slope and judging by the sound, it seemed to be coming straight for us. Eventually it appeared to one side at a distance of perhaps a hundred feet. In the same instant that we saw it, the bear put on his brakes. Madly braking against the slope he was propelled by his own momentum another hundred and fifty feet before he could stop. There he stood, his nose in the air, sniffing back and forth and looking down into the valley. Clearly he could smell us but didn't know that we were behind him. He continued to sniff and look for several minutes. This incident impressed on me the bear's amazing sense of smell. Even racing down a hill at great speed this bear was instantly aware of our scent. He knew we were near even from a distance and even though he could neither see us nor hear us.

Bears are curious animals and will come to investigate odd smells. Perfumes and cosmetics are strange smells to a bear. Although there is no current evidence that bears are attracted to menstruating women, the prudent thing is to use tampons rather than pads and to dispose of used tampons as one would food: burn completely or seal in a plastic bag and carry out.

After proper food selection comes proper food packaging. Many of the foods you bring will be factory sealed: granola bars, cereal, pasta dishes. It certainly doesn't hurt to double bag this food inside plastic bags. Trail mix, fruit, tea bags, etc. should all be double bagged in plastic. And don't forget all those other interesting smells in the pack: toothpaste, sunscreen, and skin lotion. Bag everything. It keeps each item dry in wet weather and it avoids bear problems. Food should ideally be stored in an outside pouch which is strapped to the main pack. This means that food smells do not get into the main pack. There is often difficulty in putting the whole pack in a cache as a fifty pound pack is too heavy for many branches. At night the main pack will be kept in one place and the food pouch can be strung up in a tree. If a bear does go after the food, and gets it, the rest of the gear will be safe.

It is even more important not to attract bears to the tent. Food should never be stored, eaten or cooked in the tent. Food residue or odors on skin or clothing is the same as having food in the tent. Bears can be attracted to any odor including toothpaste. Tents now come with vestibules and hikers are sometimes using these as bad weather kitchens and maulings have resulted. People who mountaineer or winter camp may not have concerns about bear safety. In that case they can consider having one tent which will have food smells on it while keeping a second tent for travel in bear country.

Philip Torrens and Mark Hill knew they were in bear country. They were concerned enough to take a shotgun for protection. On the Arctic coast east of the Mackenzie River delta, both grizzlies and polar bears can be expected. They knew they should not eat or cook in their tent but sometimes took chances. It was cold even though it was early August and the wind blew steadily. Above treeline there was no escape from the wind except in the tent. The wind made it hard to operate the campstove and quickly cooled the food. For a couple of weeks, Philip and Mark had been cooking in the vestibule of their tent and eating inside.

Earlier in the day they had stopped at a DEW line camp and been invited to stay for supper. When they left they were given a present: half a cooked chicken wrapped in aluminum foil. Traveling on for a few more miles they set up the tent, crawled inside and ate the chicken. After finishing their snack, they buried the chicken bones well away from camp: about 500 ft (150 m). Then they tried to get the worst of the chicken grease off their fingers before going to bed. There is a lot of condensation inside a tent and that isn't good for a shotgun. On this particular night they decided to protect the shotgun by keeping it inside its waterproof case. Usually they slept with the shotgun between them but somehow the shotgun ended up between Philip and his side of the tent.

When the bear attacked, it attacked from Philip's side. Swiping at them through the side of the tent, it caught Philip in the face and spun him over. Barely able to see without his glasses, Philip struggled to free himself from his sleeping bag, find the gun, and get it out of the case. The bear raked Philip's foot with its teeth and gave him a second blow with his claws. When it paused, Mark grabbed the gun, chambered a round, and fired through the tent wall. The bear was gone, Philip was injured, and their trip was over.

Even without the bear safety issue, cooking in a tent is a bad idea for a number of reasons. Stoves burn oxygen and produce carbon monoxide. Carbon monoxide is colorless and odorless and continues to build in the blood stream even after exposure. It is ultimately fatal. Tent-cooking can also be dangerous because stoves do tip over and occasionally burst into flames. Flames will dissolve tent material. Why risk the loss of your tent? Take extra food which doesn't require cooking. This provides an option during bad weather to quickly eat and get in the tent. If the only food available for supper needs cooking, then in bad weather one may be tempted to cook in the tent.

When cooking, cook only what will be eaten. There should be no leftovers. If there are, burn the food and packaging completely or put it in a plastic bag and dispose of it later. Burying the food does not work. The bear's sense of smell is too great for that.

Dishes, cutlery, and pots, should be washed as soon as the meal is over. In a wilderness setting, it may be permissible to wash dishes in large fast flowing streams, well away from camp. Remember: dishes downstream and water supply upstream. If the water is flowing, the food will be diluted and dispersed. At high elevation there is little biological activity in the water and this is not an acceptable option. Food scraps will be there for a long time. If you have dishwater to dispose of, dump it a long way and downwind from the tents. Store dishes and cutlery with the food; just in case the dish washing is less than perfect.

Cooking should be downwind and away from the tent and always wash hands after cooking. If food has been on your clothing, do not wear this clothing to bed. By following these suggestions you should have little reason to expect bear visitors.

The final step is to cache your food. If you are car camping, your cache is your car trunk. If you are in a park and a cache is provided, this should be a warning. Be sure to use it. The caches are platforms built higher than a bear can reach. Wooden poles are clad in metal to prevent bears from climbing to get to the cache. If the cache has a ladder be sure to take the ladder down. Some caches involve metal poles and pulleys — like a flag being hoisted up a flag pole. Ground level bear-proof boxes are another alternative.

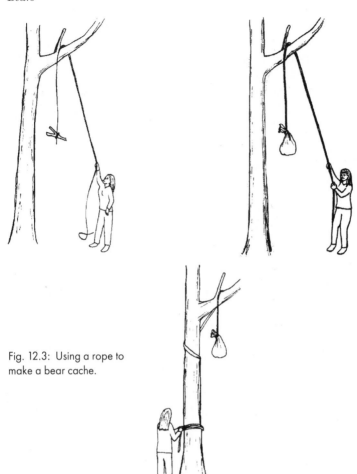

Fig. 12.3: Using a rope to make a bear cache.

When in wilderness areas, a hiker can bring cord to create their own cache. Tie one end of the cord to a thick but short stick, throw the stick over a high branch, retrieve the end of the cord with the stick, replace the stick with a food bag, and haul up the food. Bears can reach surprisingly far, so the food bag should be at least 10 ft (3 m) from the ground, and 4 ft (1 m) away from the trunk of the tree. The hauling end of the cord should be looped horizontally so the bear will not snag it should it takes a swipe at the food bag. The bag should also hang a foot or so below the branch so that small animals cannot get to the food from the branch. All of this, of course, is very theoretical. Trees ideal for the purpose are rare.

Hanging food from rafters or ceiling beams is also a good idea when using wilderness cabins. Look for mice droppings or play it safe by always hanging your pack before you go to sleep. Weasels, wolverines, squirrels and birds steal food if given the opportunity so always keep an eye on food until it is safely stashed.

A neat camp is a good policy. If your gear is properly stowed at all times, it is less interesting to animals, bears included, and is easier to keep track of.

BEAR PROTECTION

Carrying a firearm for protection from bears is problematic. A wounded, angry bear is worse than just an angry bear. In Canada, the carrying of handguns is severely restricted. A large caliber rifle or shotgun combined with proper knowledge and training is the best alternative. The gun of choice for bear protection is the 12 gauge shotgun loaded with a rifled slug. This will add a minimum of 6 pounds to your pack. Carrying a gun in your hands or across your chest in a safari sling is inconvenient. A gun strapped to your pack will not be immediately available. Guns are highly effective but not a practical solution for hikers.

Pepper spray (also called capsicum spray) is becoming a popular alternative. It is legal in parks, lightweight, and can be accessed in seconds without removing the pack. It can be carried in a holster hung from your belt or attached to your pack's front carrying strap. Experience has shown bear spray to be effective most of the time. Unfortunately, it is only useful at very close quarters, 10 to 20 ft (3 to 6 m). Check the manufacturer's specifications on the label. Because it is a spray, it is vulnerable to wind. Ideal conditions would be no wind or wind blowing from behind you and towards the bear. The spray must strike the bear in the face to be effective. The effect on the bear lasts approximately 10 minutes, after which bears have been known to approach again. If forced to use spray, do not assume that the incident is over. Use the time during which the bear is recovering from the spray to seek safety or leave the area. Some critics argue that if a mauling ensues the pepper spray may be transferred from the bear's fur to the victim, making the victim writhe and be unable to "play dead." Nevertheless, we know that in bear attack situations where spray has been used, bears have broken off attacks and maulings have been averted.

Note the date that the bear spray was bought or manufactured. Spray typically has a useful life of three years after which a replacement canister should be purchased. If flying advise the pilot that you are carrying bear spray and follow his directions. The accidental release of the spray in a small plane could incapacitate the pilot.

Fig. 12.4: Bear protection.

The use of starter guns, strike flares, distress flares and bear bangers is based on the assumption that the attack victim can frighten the bear away. This will not always work. Even high-powered rifle shots are not always enough to scare a bear away.

Consider bear bangers. They are even lighter and smaller than bear spray. The bear banger is a tube the size of a small pen which is hand held. A spring inside the tube is compressed by thumb action. When released the spring pushes a firing pin to one end of the tube. The firing pin makes contact with the bear banger cartridge which is screwed into the end of the tube. A small charge propels the cartridge into the air where the cartridge explodes. It sounds like a gunshot. Hopefully the bear will run from the shot. If the bear is close, the shot should be fired overhead rather than at it. If the cartridge lands on the far side of the bear, the bear is likely to run towards you rather than away from you. In an emergency, a flare can be inserted in the banger in place of the exploding cartridge. It is a good distress signal.

In a tent, a personal alarm of the kind sold to discourage muggers may be useful. Small, lightweight, and at 110 to 120 decibels enough to startle both furry and human attackers.

BEAR HYSTERIA

I do not believe a book on hiking would be complete without a discussion of bear behavior and bear encounter strategies. At the same time, I do not want to cause the reader undue alarm. I have spent my adult life hiking in bear country. In my first summer in British Columbia, I can recall climbing out of one of the beautiful inlets that pierce Vancouver Island's west coast. We climbed rocky outcroppings that afforded views of the inlet. When we finally reached a point with a truly panoramic view, I looked down to see a spot which had only moments before been vacated by a resting bear. I felt to see if it was still warm. The bear must have chosen this spot just as we had done. It had watched and listened as we climbed the slope, and finally, just before we arrived, had slipped away into the bush.

Over the years I have often wondered how many times bears have stood quietly and unseen watching me go by. The times I have seen them at close quarter must be the exceptions. Those times I caught them unaware. Usually the bear is already taking flight: their great bulk crashing through the brush with the finesse of a cannon ball. These were typically bears encountered near roads or settlements. The wilder the country, the less likely I have been to have a bear stare back at me. At no time have I ever felt myself threatened. Bears are often more afraid of us than we are of them.

People are mauled by bears each year and there are occasional fatalities. When compared to the number of deaths from hypothermia or drowning, the numbers are insignificant. The possibility of attack by bear, nevertheless, excites the imagination. Hopefully the reader will use the information in this chapter to reduce the fear quotient to an acceptable level. By following good food handling practices, hikers will contribute to their own safety as well as the safety of those who follow.

THE COUGAR OR MOUNTAIN LION

The cougar or mountain lion lives throughout most of North and South America. The largest recorded was an Arizona cougar which weighed 276 pounds (125 kg). More typically adult males are in the 140 to 200 pound (64 to 90 kg) range with females between 90 and 120 pounds (41 to 55 kg). The cougar's main food is deer although they will kill and eat whatever is available: from mice to moose.

Cougar attacks are not common. There have been 34 recorded cougar attacks in British Columbia in the past 100 years. Five of them fatal. Children are at increased risk since most of those attacked have been children. California has the most acute cougar problem. There the number of cougars has more than doubled in the 20 years since a hunting ban was imposed.

Cougars are elusive animals which generally avoid contact with humans and are rarely seen. They are far less of a hazard than bears although not as well understood. Much of what has already been said about bears applies to cougars. Avoid cougar kills unless armed. Do not approach cougar kits. Make noises or travel in groups. Cougars are more likely to attack children than adults and more likely to attack an individual than a party of two or more. If you see a cougar do not try to run. If confronted try to convince the cougar that you are a threat and not prey by enlarging your image. Stand tall. Wave your arms or a branch. If attacked do not play dead. Fight for your life.

13.

BITERS AND CRAWLERS

One of the inevitable and more disagreeable parts of many hiking trips are the biting insects. Insects are the most pervasive and successful of all animals — there are more species of insects alive in the world than of all other animals combined. The good news is that in the United States and Canada, there are relatively few diseases spread by insects. There are techniques for minimizing the misery they bring but there are no complete solutions. A bit of understanding goes a long way.

Here is a list of the pest insects we will consider (see Chapter 6 for a discussion of deer mice and hantavirus pulmonary syndrome);

1. mosquitoes, blackflies, horseflies, deerflies, biting midges
2. ticks
3. bees, wasps, and hornets
4. spiders

MOSQUITOES, BLACKFLIES AND OTHER BITING FLIES

Mosquitoes, blackflies, biting midges (no-see-ums), horseflies, deerflies, and snipe flies have at least two things in common. They all bite humans and they are all members of the order Diptera. I will refer to them all simply as biting flies although mosquitoes and blackflies cause the most problems. There are approximately 160 species of mosquitoes in the US and 74 species in Canada[1]. Canada has over one hundred species of blackflies[2]. Only a few blackfly species will take human blood. The number of biting fly species seems large but is, in fact, smaller than the number of species that are found in tropical countries. Still the sheer numbers of biting flies at certain times and in certain places can be nothing short of astounding. In areas of the Arctic, mosquito and blackfly populations explode for short periods during the brief northern summer. Almost all of the biting flies require water to complete their life cycle and this type of habitat is abundantly available in the far north country. The climaxing population of biting flies far exceeds the ability of parasites and predators to dent their numbers.

The biting flies may overwinter as eggs, larva, or as adults waiting for the coming spring. It is difficult to predict the date on which they will emerge as pests. In any location, there will be year to year variations depending on the onset of spring-like weather. Different species will emerge at different times throughout the spring and summer. In general, the further north, the later the arrival of spring weather and the later the appearance of biting flies. On the Arctic islands, mosquitoes do not usually appear until July. Mosquitoes bite man and animal alike, seeking blood as a necessary source of protein for the development of their eggs. It is the female that is the problem. The male does not need blood and does not bite.

Biting flies have a highly developed ability to detect carbon dioxide and will follow it to its source. The fly will also respond to body heat and moisture given off by its animal or human prey. Exertion increases carbon dioxide as well as heat and moisture thereby attracting more flying pests. Biting flies can detect and may be attracted to certain odors: deodorants, soaps with fragrances, toothpaste, or chewing gum. Sound does not appear to have much effect. At close range, vision comes into play and it has been found that dark colors are most attractive to biting flies. Perhaps this is because dark colors more closely resemble the fur of their usual animal targets.

Once the mosquito has landed, taste receptors on its feet come into contact with the skin. Experience tells us that two people may be standing next to each other and one person may get bitten more often than the other. The mosquito seems to make a last minute deliberation based on a chemical analysis of the host's skin before deciding whether to feed or not. When feeding, the mosquito pierces the skin and probes about for a capillary. It has the ability to inject saliva into its host at the same time as it is pumping out the blood. The saliva acts as an anticoagulant. The mosquito's saliva is allergenic and the body reacts by creating the characteristic swelling and itch.

Blackflies often crawl about looking for a sheltered place to bite; the hairline, openings in clothing, or behind the ears. Black flies do not bite out chunks of skin, (although it may feel that way), but snip the skin and let the blood flow. That is why a blackfly bite will leave a small residual drop of blood on the skin. Scratching seems to make the itch worse and may cause secondary infection.

The midge, or no-see-um, is the smallest of the biting flies and snips the skin like a blackfly. Its bite creates a burning sensation. Horseflies and deerflies occur south of the treeline particularly in the boreal forests where there are large, boggy areas. Their bite is particularly painful. There are a host of other biting flies which feed on animals to the exclusion of man.

Man has been searching for ways to combat the flying hordes for millennia. The first Europeans called the natives "red men" because they mistook the red ochre that they wore as mosquito protection for true skin color. Today we still smear our skin with all manner of things.

Smoky fires, or smudges, are a traditional and effective way to keep biting insects at bay. The Natives lit smudges indoors on the earth floor of their tepees. A smoky campfire is still a good way to find relief. Each camper must strike a balance between need for relief and the discomfort of smoke stinging their eyes and permeating their clothing.

Relief from blackflies comes at night when they cease to bite. During the day favorite feeding times are early morning and early evening. Trapped inside a vehicle or tent they tend not to bite and focus their energy on escaping from confinement rather than eating. Mosquitoes and no-see-ums offer no respite when the sun goes down and continue their attack. Many hikers avoid the early, warm spring temperatures when mosquitoes are known to be hungry. Blackflies do not necessarily appear at the same time as mosquitoes. That depends on how they overwinter and the temperature of the rivers from which they emerge. To the south they may precede the mosquitoes. In Alaska, the Yukon, and the Northwest Territories, they may not emerge until the mosquitoes have almost disappeared. By late August or September when cool nights return most biting flies break off the attack. This adds an extra appeal to late summer and fall hiking. Indian summer brings fall colors of reds and yellows, fewer humans, cooler temperatures, lovely days, and no bugs.

Biting flies require calm air or gentle breezes to do their work. A bit of wind brings relief for man and animal. Hiking along an exposed ridge is likely to be better than hiking through thick vegetation in the valley. Biting flies begin to fly when they emerge from ponds, marshes, and wetlands as winged adults and the females begin their hunt for blood. They can travel several kilometers but if wet places are avoided, we can avoid the worst of the flies. While mosquitoes favor still water, blackflies require moving water and are therefore associated more with streams than ponds. When looking for a campsite, choose a spot which is open and swept by breezes. A tent pitched in the trees may be protected from windstorms but should be avoided if the weather is fair and bugs are about. A spit projecting out into a lake or an exposed hilltop will catch whatever breezes blow and will be the first place that the flies abandon.

Clothing is the first line of defense against biting flies. Loose-fitting, nylon clothing is superior to woven fabrics like cotton. Rain gear is perfect to discourage bugs although not always very comfortable in warm weather. Beware the places where clothes meet as blackflies will crawl through. Tuck in the shirt and pull socks over pant cuffs. Zippers are better than buttons. For those venturing into the Alaskan or Canadian north during the height of the bug season, extreme precautions may be considered. Specially designed bug jackets, shirts, pants, gaiters, and headnets are all available from outdoor stores. These pants and gaiters have stirrups. Push the feet into shoes or boots and the bottoms of the gaiters or pants pull down and over the ankles to protect them. Bug jackets and bug shirts each have a mesh head net attached — beekeeper fashion. It is intended that a brimmed hat will be worn under the head net. This keeps the netting away from the hair and skin and the insects cannot reach through the mesh. For the last word in bug protection, choose a spray insecticide containing permethrin. The permethrin is sprayed on the bug clothing and will kill both blackflies and mosquitoes.

For decades, researchers have been searching for a better bug dope. Folklore is full of traditional remedies: smeared urine, garlic, mud, eucalyptus, vitamin B, citronella and citrus fruits. Of these, citronella has been found to have a negligible effect. Some people claim that Avon's Skin-So-Soft bath oil has mosquito repellent properties. Avon makes no such claim and the product contains no deet. When tested by Consumer's Union the product was found to offer little to no protection. So far there is nothing as effective as deet. Deet is the common name for diethyltoluamide and has been around since the 1950s although researchers still don't know exactly why it works. It doesn't kill the insects. In fact it doesn't even make them go away. They will continue to swarm about, but they do not bite. Deet is the active ingredient in an array of insect repellents. When picking a repellent, check the contents on the label. Look for deet under its chemical name. The greater the percentage of deet the greater the repellent's effectiveness. The higher too will be its toxicity. The maximum recommended deet concentration is 50 percent and substantially less for children. The compound may irritate the skin of some people and have a neurological effect on others. Deet should be used sparingly, a little at a time and not at all on young children and pregnant women. Avoid applying it near the eyes, lips, open cuts, or near food. If using a spray, don't apply directly to the face but spray your hands and then wipe your face and neck. Solvents which are combined with the deet have a harmful effect on synthetics: Spandex, vinyl, nylon, rayon, acetate, and particularly plastics. Deet will dissolve plastics so be careful with eyeglass frames, and watch crystals. Some formulations are flammable. Deet loses its effectiveness after a few hours and must be reapplied. Sweating will wash it from the skin's surface. If mosquitoes are expected take a small bottle of liquid bug dope. If canoe camping and weight is not a major concern bring deet in spray form. Spray bug dope is useful when applied to clothing, particularly shirt and pant cuffs as well as on tent netting.

In general approach bug protection with a 'least is best' philosophy. If there is a choice of dates try to avoid entering areas at a time when biting flies are at their worst. A few bites are not a terrible thing and should be tolerated. Powerful bug spray should only be used when insects are overly abundant. Tolerate a few bites and over time see if the body adjusts. Preparations such as "After Bite" will help to ease the itching until your body has built up its level of tolerance. Unfortunately tolerance to one species of biting fly in one location will not necessarily increase the body's tolerance to another species at a different location.

Researchers have found that biting insects identify certain locations where they will swarm in great numbers. These swarms are primarily males. They pick a prominent object as a "swarm marker" and this will be where they spend most of their time. If hiking into a swarm of mosquitoes don't automatically reach for the deet. Try moving a distance away from them and seeing if the insects follow.

TICKS AND LYME DISEASE

Lyme disease was first diagnosed at Lyme, Connecticut, in the mid 1970s. Although it is still concentrated in the northeastern United States or mid-Atlantic region, it has been found across the continent and around the world. Tick populations vary widely across North America from location to location and between different tick populations the risk of tick borne disease varies greatly. Some tick populations are highly infected by the bacteria which cause Lyme disease while others have little or no disease. The level of tick disease is, however, increasing, so keeping up to date with the degree of risk in a given area is important. Consult local health boards for current information concerning tick infestation in your area. The deer mouse and some other rodents are the reservoir for bacteria which is spread by ticks to other animal hosts. Ticks which do not carry Lyme disease may carry other diseases: relapsing fever, tularemia, and Rocky Mountain spotted fever among them.

The symptoms of Lyme disease are similar to those of many other diseases which makes it a difficult disease for doctors to diagnose. The good news is that effective treatment is available if the disease is diagnosed early. Early symptoms occur within the first month of being bitten. These are general flu-like symptoms: headache, fatigue, joint pain, and chills and often a spreading rash at the place bitten. If the disease is not diagnosed and treated, it can lie dormant before emerging months or even years later. The later symptoms include arthritic-like joint problems, heart ailments, as well as neurological damage which can manifest itself in a range of psychiatric problems: depression, panic attacks, memory problems, and psychotic-like disorders.

Detecting ticks is difficult because they are small: from the size of a dot to 3/16 of an inch (4mm) long. When feeding on blood, they become engorged and may become many times their normal size. The tick will wait for an animal host on grass or in vegetation, and, when an animal or human passes by, will attach itself to the skin, cut a hole, and burrow into the skin. The mouth will be under the skin while the rest of its body sticks out. As it sucks in blood its body swells. After it has finished it will drop off the host. Infected ticks will leave disease behind in the bloodstream of the host. A skin rash may appear and, in about half of those bitten, the rash will have a characteristic bull's eye appearance.

Not all ticks carry disease. Check to determine if you will be traveling through an area where ticks will be present and if those ticks are likely to carry disease. If so, choose to stay on cleared trails rather than traveling through tall grass or brushy areas. Protect skin with clothing. Tuck your shirt into your pants and tuck your pants into your socks. Pants with elasticized cuffs are better than loose cuffs as they protect the lower leg and do not snag on the underbrush. Tests, conducted by Consumer Reports magazine have shown deet to be ineffective in repelling deer ticks. If sufficiently concerned about tick borne disease, spray an insecticide containing permethrin on clothing, sleeping bags and tents. Permethrin will also kill mosquitoes and biting flies on contact. Inspect yourself when in tick country and if you find that a tick has attached, do not make the situation worse by breaking off the body and leaving the mouth under the skin, or squeezing the tick and re-circulating the blood back into your body. Tweezers or a loop of thread will help you to get hold of the tick as close to the skin as possible. Pull the tick straight out. Use a knife to scrape away any remaining mouth parts. If you have no tweezers and decide to use your fingers, protect bare fingers with a plastic bag. If the mouth is embedded in the skin, the tick may be encouraged to back out by being touched with a hot but extinguished match head. If in an area with tick borne diseases, save the tick for testing by a local health board. The broken skin and fingers should be washed with soap. Seek medical advice if you develop a characteristic bull's eye rash.

BEES, WASPS, AND HORNETS

Bees, wasps, and hornets should not be swatted. If they or their hive is not in danger they are unlikely to sting. The hiker's greatest danger is in inadvertently blundering into a nest. Usually the first hiker disturbs the nest as he walks by and those following get attacked. This is a good reason to step over logs rather than jarring them by stepping on them. An attack by a swarm of angry wasps is frightening as well as painful. Wasps and hornets can sting several times while bees sting once, leaving their barbed stingers embedded in the skin. Wasps mark their stings with a substance that encourages other nest defenders to attack. Move away from the vicinity and wash the affected area as soon as possible. Bee stingers remaining in the skin should be scraped off with a knife. Using fingers or tweezers will tend to squeeze the venom sack attached to the stinger and pump venom into the wound. There will be swelling and redness. Some people may have a general allergic reaction: difficulty in breathing, weakness, vomiting and collapse. Those with a known severe allergic response should be carrying epinephrine with them. Antihistamines, particularly Benadryl, will be of use for milder allergic responses. All hikers should consider adding antihistamine tablets to the first aid kit.

SPIDERS

In the United States and Canada several spiders have venom which produce neurotoxic symptoms. Of these, the black widow spider is best known. The black widow is black and shiny with a crimson spot on the underside of its abdomen. The females are up to half an inch in length. The species gets its name from the mistaken belief that the female kills the male after mating. The largest populations of black widow spiders occur in California. They are small, shy, nocturnal creatures which spend their days in dark locations. Although there have been fatalities from this spider, it is now believed to be far less of a menace than previously thought. Small children and the elderly are most at risk. Statistically, one's chance of being fatally bitten by a black widow spider is much less than being struck by lightning.

---

1   Agriculture Canada, *Biting Flies Attacking Man and Livestock in Canada*

2   Agriculture Canada, *Black Flies*

14.

GEAR

When I began hiking several decades ago, there were few speciality outdoor hiking stores. Most hikers dressed the same way hunters or foresters did. Canvas tents were common and are still in use because they stand up well to wind and rain. Unfortunately, their weight makes them better suited to travel by horse or dogsled than backpack. Internal frame packs are of recent origin. The old standby was the Trapper Nelson pack. It had a wooden frame with a canvas bag attached. Like all external frame packs, the bag could be taken off and a load tied directly to the frame. The concept of a hip belt to take the weight of the pack was unknown. The shoulder straps were not padded and they bit into the shoulders — a painful burden! Trapper Nelsons are still in use and when metal tube frames were introduced the old timers sneered, they argued that if a wooden frame pack were broken, it could be fixed in the bush while a broken metal frame would likely stay broken.

Leather boots leaked in wet weather and rubber boots collected perspiration in dry weather, breathable hiking gear was unknown. Winter jaunts often meant jeans soaked through and the skin of the legs red and so cold they hurt. With similar hiking gear the sourdoughs flooded the Yukon and Alaska by the thousands over mountain ranges and along unmapped rivers and valleys. Most made it but some died of starvation, drowning, and hypothermia.

This is mentioned merely as a reminder that much of what the modern hiker regards as essential probably didn't exist several decades ago. In a world of rising expectations, we strive for increased comfort and convenience.

There are, however, certain basics which are a prerequisite for safe wilderness travel. When the gold seekers climbed the Chilkoot Pass on their way to the Klondike, they carried their gear in stages. They made many trips carrying 100 to 200 pounds (45 to 90 kg) each trip. They were met at the Canadian border by the RCMP who insisted that only those with a year's supplies should proceed. What should a recreational hiker carry to proceed?

WALKING STICKS

Novice hikers can often be spotted literally half a mile away. These are the individuals seen far from their cars on a sunny day sporting shorts and T-shirt, a lunch, and a camera. They are more likely to be seen carrying a walking stick than a map and compass.

There may be persons with physical disabilities who require the use of a walking stick or ski poles. For the able-bodied, such paraphernalia should not be a substitute for proper hiking technique. Ski poles have their place. For backcountry skiers and snowshoers they are an aid to balance and help propel the torso forward. The bush is full of sticks and the hiker need not bring his own. They are well supplied along rivers where their use for fording is unquestioned. A long stick can be used to walk tightrope fashion across a log and a short stick is good for catching snakes. Apart from these limited circumstances, a hiker's hands should be free. When the going gets really rough: clambering over rocks and up steep slopes, a stick is more of a hindrance than a help and one is likely to impale oneself on it. A hiker's hands should be available to protect himself from branches and underbrush, to pull himself up and over obstacles, for route finding with map and compass, and to catch himself should he stumble.

SHORTS VS. PANTS

The North American natives wore leggings to protect themselves from injury. These were made from a single piece of buckskin for each leg and were held in place by a loop through a belt worn at the waist. This type of extra leg protection was adopted by the pioneers who also wore leggings, secured at the knee by a garter.

Cowboys wore leather chaps: leather pants without the seat, and designed as extra leg protection.

The novice hiker often dispenses with leg protection completely by wearing shorts. Particularly at higher elevations, pants provide protection from the sun where there is less atmosphere to filter out UV rays. On the trail, sweat will wash sunscreen and bug dope away. On a multi-day hike where there is nowhere to wash properly, who wants a build up of lotions on the body? Biting insects love bare flesh. Prickles and branches tear at the legs rather than glancing off cloth-protected skin and on open ridges the wind can quickly suck away body heat.

If none of these considerations apply, by all means wear shorts — but carry a pair of pants in your pack just in case. My personal preference is 100 percent nylon pants because they are light, tough, relatively windproof, and dry with amazing speed. The redeeming feature of shorts is that they are cooler than pants and occasionally one encounters hikers who favor shorts and gaiters in warm, wet weather preferring bare skin to rain gear.

Cotton is a wonderfully comfortable material for clothing. It is soft against the skin and absorbs moisture from the body. At the beach, a cotton shirt soaked in water is a good way to stay cool. It has the advantage of holding lots of water in the fabric, being slow to dry, and cooling the body as the water evaporates. These advantages become serious disadvantages in the bush. In the bush a combination of damp cotton and wind or cool temperatures can quickly lower body temperature to dangerous levels. Jeans are 100 percent cotton and should be avoided. The less cotton the better with no cotton being best of all. Choose synthetic fibres: nylon, polypropylene, etc.

RAIN PANTS AND RAIN JACKETS

Breathable rain gear is widely used and manufacturers are making it attractive and fashionable. It should be noted, however, that construction workers, loggers, and others who spend their working hours outside have not adopted breathable rainwear. Why would weekenders but not outdoor workers adopt the new fabric? The truth is that the breathability feature is a trade-off with other important factors. For absolute waterproofing, maximum abrasion resistance, low maintenance, and low cost, traditional rainwear is still best. Coated nylon and rubber clothing is unquestionably waterproof and stands up better to glissading down snowy slopes, pushing through thorns and heavy brush, and scraping against rocks. In thick underbrush, prickles will pierce the breathable lining of modern materials leaving small pin holes. Breathable outerwear is a big investment. If brambles lie ahead, take off your expensive outerwear and put on the cheap stuff. Breathable fabrics are far from indestructible.

The advantage of breathable garments is that water will not penetrate from the outside in but water vapor produced by the body will pass through the garment to the outside. There are, however, limits to what a breathable material can do. Under actual trail conditions, the body can sweat faster than the fabric can vent the moisture. Do not expect miracles: only an improvement over unbreathable fabrics.

Liquids will not pass through the fabric. Rain will not come in but neither will sweat go out. If sweat builds up on the inside of your garment, the sweat will be a barrier to the water vapor escaping through the material. Breathable rainwear has then become no better than the non-breathable kind and condensation can form on its inside surface. If the material becomes wet on the outside, the result will be the same. The material will have "wetted out" and no longer be breathable.

When rainwear is first purchased, water will bead on the outer surface and quickly run away. The preservation of this essential characteristic is what proper maintenance is all about. Regular washing of the garment is recommended as dirt impedes performance. The application of heat will restore the beading feature of Gore-Tex fabrics. Tumble dry in a dryer at low heat then iron at the low steam setting. After extended use further steps may be necessary to restore the garments water-shedding ability. Products are available in outdoor stores to add to the wash cycle. The garment can be further treated with a water repelling spray when dry. Wash, iron, and spray before all major hikes.

Breathable fabrics are an evolving technology. Check the stores for the latest products and pay attention to the warranties offered. Are they limited to a few years or are they extended to the useful life of the garment?

HEAD COVERINGS

Hats, hoods and other head coverings are an essential piece of outdoor equipment. When clothed at least 20 percent of the body's heat loss is from the head. If the body cools, warm blood leaves the extremities in order to maintain the core temperature. The head is not an extremity. The brain must maintain its core temperature and the body will continue to heat the head in spite of rapid heat loss.

Hats are available for every conceivable weather condition. As a general standby a light-weight waterproof hat with a brim all around is the basic requirement. Waterproofing is important. A rain soaked hat does not effectively prevent heat loss. The brim protects the face, ears, and neck from the sun and is more reliable than sunscreen which will eventually wash  away with perspiration. The brim also acts to protect the face and eyes from underbrush. When there are light branches across the trail, lower the head and push through.

When it is cold as well as wet, a rubberized sou'wester, the kind associated with fishermen, is ideal. With a brim which extends backwards behind the collar, rain runs off the back brim and down the outside of the jacket. The heavy rubber coating is totally waterproof and provides reasonable insulation.

Hoods do an even better job of keeping the neck and head dry in miserable conditions such as driving rain or snow, but they do not commonly have a brim and restrict one's vision and hearing to the sides.

Below freezing, when conditions are dry, use a toque. The thicker insulating layers retain body heat well. The toque grips the head and can be worn at night in the sleeping bag for extra warmth. When the weather is at its absolute worst, cold with driving rain or snow, a toque worn under a hood provides maximum weather protec-

tion. A balaclava protects the face from extreme cold.

FIRST AID KIT

Hikers are people who go to great lengths to reduce the size and weight of the gear they must carry: saving a fraction of an ounce by chopping off handles of tooth brushes and spending top dollar to have the latest lightweight tent. When compromises are being made, the first aid kit is one of the first places likely to be cut. Trip leaders will often carry first aid kits due to legal liability or insurance requirements. If the medical history or physical condition of participants is not known a greater range of medical emergencies must be anticipated. Children may have undiagnosed sensitivities to insect bites. In the backcountry we become responsible for each other and must accept each other on an "as is" basis and be prepared for almost anything.

It is ironic that on day hikes when medical help is closest, a full first aid kit is not a great burden, while on multi-day hikes when help is least available packs are already full and heavy. Thankfully, only one first aid kit is necessary and the weight of it can be shared. One leader can carry the stove or extra food to ease the load for the person carrying the first aid kit. A good first aid kit, however, is not a substitute for first aid knowledge and in a medical emergency a cool head and knowledge of first aid is the key. As a minimum, anyone who is responsible for children should have a current standard, or wilderness, first aid certificate.

Careful thought should go into the components of a first aid kit. Don't assume that there is a "standard" first aid kit or that any first aid kit will do. You may prefer to take the extra time to assemble your own kit, placing in it the items which you feel are the most appropriate for the particular trip and the needs of the participants. Begin with the medical condition of the participants. What medical problems do they have? If those problems flare up will they have their pills, braces, or other supplies with them? Is the first aid kit capable of handling the medical emergencies which are most likely to occur? All of the following are available individually from first aid supply houses. Are they appropriate for your needs?

foot care (see Chapter 7):
  – moleskin (Dr. Scholl's Kurotex)
  – Dr. Scholl's Molefoam
  – 2nd Skin Moist Burn Pad (Spenco Medical Corp.)
  – small nail scissors

sun protection:
- sunscreen
- lip block
- sunglasses

skin care:
- hand lotion
- lip balm

insect protection (see Chapter 13):
- bug dope containing deet
- After Bite for treatment of insect bite irritation in children or those with sensitive skin
- Benadryl, an antihistamine to treat allergic responses to insect stings
- tweezers to remove ticks, and to clean open wounds

small wounds
- band aids particularly flexible fabric dressings which can be cut to the desired size and shape
- butterfly bandages to close wounds in place of stitches
- antibiotic ointment (e.g. Polysporin) to prevent infection

large wounds
- sterile abdominal pad or field dressing
- sterile pads for wound cleaning and dressing
- 1" and 2" regular bandages
- antiseptic sterile towels for cleaning wounds (e.g. benzalkonium chloride towelettes)
- adhesive tape
- scissors (see foot care above)

breaks, dislocations, and sprains
- triangular bandages with safety.pins
- tensor bandage with clamps
- flexible folding splint (or SAM splint)

shock and hypothermia
- emergency space blanket for immobilized subjects
- aspirin to treat cold injuries in adults (see Chapter 15)

other
- bar soap
- analgesic for pain

- pocket mask with one way valve for avoiding infection when administering mouth to mouth resuscitation
- latex gloves for personal protection when touching blood or other bodily fluids
- a basic first aid guide

GEARING UP

Getting ready for a multi-day hike takes time and planning. It is a challenge to reduce one's essentials to a size and weight one can comfortably carry. Difficult choices must be made. There will be no opportunity to return for a forgotten item or go to the store.

Prepare gradually. First comes the logistics. Is the trip feasible? What can be learned from maps, guide books, or people who know the area? If feasible, how long will it take? What weather can be expected?

The answers to these questions will begin to suggest what gear will be necessary. There is no standard gear. The gear depends on the trip, experience, and personal preference. The following are the basics:

Maps in waterproof covers: Absolutely essential. A 1:50,000 is fine. If hiking a long way you may be able to get by with fewer maps by buying smaller scale maps. See Chapter 2.

Compass: Don't set foot on the trail without one. Know how to use a compass. See Chapter 3.

Watch: See Chapter 4.

Pack: Wait till you see what gear you are carrying before you choose a pack. A big expedition pack has lots of places to strap on gear and a comfortable hip belt. Food is strapped to the outside of the pack. It is difficult to get a properly sized day pack, many are too small.

Clothing: Follow the layering principal. Plan to change clothing throughout the day. The body will generate varying amounts of heat according to the level of exertion. Moving from sun to shade or from a windy to a sheltered place will all effect comfort levels. Many thin layers provide more options than a few heavy ones. Thin polypropylene layers next to the skin are warm and dry quickly. Nylon shirts and pants dry quickly and cut the wind's chill. Fleece shirts, vests, and jackets are light, warm, and also dry quickly. Carry extra clothing in waterproof plastic bags so that there is a change of clothing in case of rain, dew, perspiration, or immersion.

Head covering: Sun and bad weather headgear.

Rain gear: Jacket, gaiters, pants and hat. Ventilated rainwear with zip vents at the armpits help to direct water vapor away from the body.

Boots, liner socks, and hiking socks: See Chapter 7.

Headlamp: On day hikes plan for the possibility that you may be delayed. Better sometimes to hike in darkness than spend the night. On overnight trips always have a flashlight or headlamp.

Camp shoes: Preferably running shoes over sandals. See Chapter 7.

Mole skin and scissors to treat blisters: The scissors are useful for keeping toenails trimmed as well as cutting moleskin. See Chapter 7.

Gaiters

Food: Lightweight, dry food with short cooking times for multi-day trips. For day trips favorites are: apples, pears, carrots, trail mix, and granola bars. See Chapter 10.

Stove, spare fuel, metal plate, cutlery and cup: A plastic measuring cup when camping, both for drinking as well as measuring ingredients. A table knife isn't much use. Take a pocket knife or sheathed knife instead.

Water: Always carry water in the winter when surface water is likely to be frozen. See Chapter 11 for a full discussion of this important topic.

Matches: Carried inside an empty film canister.

Toilet paper: In double plastic bags.

Sleeping bag: A synthetic fill sleeping bag is heavier and bulkier but will do a superior job of keeping you warm when your bag gets wet.

Tent: Don't go for the smallest and lightest if it won't protect you from strong winds and rain. That means a fly which extends down to the ground and has lots of tie-downs.

Bear spray: See Chapter 12.

Toiletries: Toothbrush, toothpaste, etc.

Pen and paper

Skin protection: Bug dope, sunscreen, lip block, hand cream.

Sunglasses

First aid supplies

Rope: For repairs and to hang the food bag.

Fewer compromises are necessary when preparing for a day hike. Without a tent, sleeping bag, and bulky food, everything needed can easily be carried. An extended trip however requires much more forethought and gear should be assembled gradually. Start assembling your gear many days before the departure date. Lay out the gear on the floor where it will all be visible and add items as you think of them. Remove items as you make compromises. Try fitting it all in the pack. Can you reasonably expect to carry the weight? Resist the last minute urge to throw in more gear on the day you leave.

THE BIG PICTURE

Regardless of the expense or quality of the gear, plan for the day that it will fail and there will be no replacement. Consider the following:

- the seam of the sleeping bag's stuff sack rips leaving you with an armful of sleeping bag and nowhere to put it.

- the stove overheats and bursts into flames, burning and destroying the seals. You are left with dry food and no way to cook it.

- Three or four days travel from the nearest road the sole of your hiking boot falls off.

- the attachment which joins the pack's carrying strap to the pack breaks. The pack can be carried by hand but not on your back.

- after pushing through heavy wet brush for days, the breathable rain gear has stopped being waterproof. You are soaked with another week to go to find shelter.

- the strap that attaches the gaiter to your boot has worn through. One gaiter is flapping about uselessly.

- a driving rain storm is keeping you awake, suddenly the tent collapses on top of you.
- while lying in the tent listening to the gentle rain you feel something wet underneath you. The place where the tent was pitched has become a puddle and water is seeping through the floor of the tent.

All of these situations have happened to me. While perfectly good gear can serve admirably for years eventually it will wear out or give way. The pack and gaiters can be fixed with cord or rope, the sleeping bag can be compressed and packaged using a section of rope. Without spare parts and tools, the stove cannot be fixed, so either share a friend's stove or revert to campfire cookery. When a boot falls apart, the running shoes brought as camp shoes can be pressed into service. When soaked from leaky rain gear switch to the extra dry clothing which always should be carried in waterproof bags. The repitching of tents in the blackness of night is never pleasant but with a flashlight can be accomplished. Remember always to pitch the tent where water will not gather and tie and stake the tent so as to lessen the risk of it collapsing if the wind comes up.

Expect the unexpected. Do you have spare parts for your stove? Should you bring a flashlight or headlamp? What about wire or cord for repairs? Redundancy is an important concept. Carry two small rolls of toilet paper, not one big one. If one gets wet you will have a spare. The same applies to matches. Separate matches in separate locations. If two people are traveling together consider whether they should both carry stoves. Ideally they would both use the same type of fuel. Are sufficient clothes being carried in case dry clothes are needed? If the compass is lost could you orient yourself with the sun? Do you have supplies to treat blisters and other minor medical emergencies?

Always consider what steps may be necessary if any item of gear fails. If going on a long hike try new gear out beforehand on short hikes. Most people know that new boots should be broken in slowly. Even then, I have been in a party where a hiker wore new boots and ended the day in agony, barely able to walk. On a three day trip a hiker tried gluing his gaiters to his boots to keep the snow out. The experiment worked but his feet became so hot on dry ground that his feet blistered and eventually bled. Try out new ideas on short hikes, but stick to the tried and true on long hikes.

This chapter will end with the story of John Colter, who completed a hike that would challenge anyone regardless of the type of gear carried. In fact John Colter carried no gear: he was naked.

In the summer of 1808, mountain man John Colter joined the Flathead and Crow Indians in their battle against the Blackfoot. When he was captured by the Blackfoot in the fall of that year he was recognized and his companion immediately killed. John was stripped entirely naked and every item of gear taken from him. A score of braves then sharpened their spears in readiness for a grim competition.

John was given a sporting head start in a race for his own life. He outran his pursuers and began a desperate struggle to reach help at Fort Manuel at the confluence of the Yellowstone and Bighorn Rivers in present day Montana. The occasional snowfall melted on his naked skin. The rocks and vegetation ripped his bare feet and legs. At night there was no shelter, blankets, or fire to warm him. He had no map or compass to guide him. He ate only what roots he could scrounge. And yet, John Colter traveled through 250 miles (400 km) of wilderness as naked and alone as any human has ever been, arriving at Fort Manuel haggard but alive eleven days later.

15.

WINTER TRAVEL

When summer ends and the weather cools, many hikers desert the trails and take up more sedentary pursuits, not realizing what they are missing. The trails and camping spots empty of people, many animals either migrate or hibernate and the usually hectic pace of the woods abates. With the changing colors and eventual snow the forest becomes a magical place. Gone are the mosquitoes and blackflies. Animal tracks in the snow are easily visible and tell stories on the forest floor. As the temperature drops below freezing, the ponds and wetlands freeze over and places can now be visited which were too wet and boggy the rest of the year. In the far north "winter roads" open up. These are primitive and remote routes through bush and bog that are only passable to overland vehicle travel when winter makes the ground firm and snow fills in the hollows and covers over the underbrush.

The hiker will discover new delights which were unavailable during the rest of the year. When the snow is soft and deep, the feet sink in and walking becomes slow and tiring. Out come the snowshoes and backcountry skis. Obstacles disappear, buried under a sea of white. The route becomes more level. There are fewer concerns about foot placement. The feet move rhythmically, oblivious to the tangled vegetation beneath the snow.

SNOWSHOES AND BACKCOUNTRY SKIS

Snowshoes were the traditional winter choice of the original North Americans. Skis were a European innovation. The snowshoe is easily mastered by any hiker but don't count on traveling as many miles as you could in summer. The snowshoe is an extra weight on each foot and the body is not accustomed to walking with the feet kept apart. The traditional snowshoe moccasin is not widely available, but most boot-gaiter combinations will do as long as the boots are warm enough. The boot is attached to the snowshoe by a snowshoe binding. Since the foot will be riding on the snowshoe frame, a heavy sole eases the pressure of the foot against the snowshoe.

There is no ideal snowshoe for all conditions. Seek guidance from staff at a speciality outdoor store. They will know what snowshoes best match the snow conditions and topography of the area. The lighter the snow, the deeper you will sink. A large snowshoe works best in soft snow especially for a heavier person. In open country with no brush to catch the snowshoe or sharp turns to manoeuvre around, a long snowshoe with a tail pointing backwards works fine. In forests with underbrush and lots of maneuvring, shorter, bear paw-shaped snowshoes are better. In mountainous terrain where steep ascents are encountered there will be a tendency to slide backwards down the slope. The traditional snowshoe allows the toe of the boot to rock down only a short way into the snow when the heel is lifted. It is not a good choice for climbing. The modern, mountaineering snowshoe has crampon-like teeth to grip the snow and provide better traction.

When wearing snowshoes, the feet must be kept slightly apart so the snowshoe of one foot does not step on the other. You must adjust your stride so as to keep the snowshoes separated. Spread your feet too wide apart and your muscles will become very sore very quickly. If the snow is firm enough, you will be able to walk without snowshoes easier than with them. Be sure to put rope in your pack so that if snow conditions change and snowshoes are not needed, you will be able to strap them to your pack. Ski poles are optional. They are useful to maintain balance in rough terrain or where obstacles are being negotiated. When going up a steep incline, a push on the poles will help propel the upper body forward.

Backcountry skiing is an alternative to snowshoeing and is a fun activity for its own sake. The backcountry skier can buy a ticket and ski the groomed downhill slopes and cross-country trails of a ski resort or escape the crowds and venture into the backcountry.

The boot of the dedicated downhill skier is firmly attached to his skis at both the toe and heel. This rigid type of binding makes all but downhill skiing difficult. The backcountry ski boot, like its cross country cousin is attached to the skis only at the toe. Backcountry ski bindings allow the heel to be raised off the ski and permits a fluid shuffling motion. When snowshoeing, the whole of the snowshoe is raised off the ground (although the tail drags on the longer styles). The backcountry skier slides but does not lift his skis. On

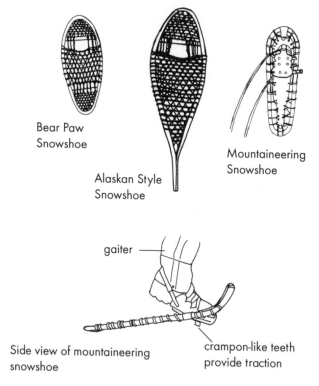

Bear Paw
Snowshoe

Alaskan Style
Snowshoe

Mountaineering
Snowshoe

gaiter

Side view of mountaineering
snowshoe

crampon-like teeth
provide traction

Fig. 15.1

level ground, he can glide forward on his skis with each step. When faced with a steep uphill climb, the backcountry skier attaches "skins" to the bottom of the skis that permit the ski to slide forward but not backwards. The snowshoer walks up and walks down. The backcountry skier walks up and slides down. No wonder skis are more popular!

If considering the purchase of backcountry skis be sure to deal with an outdoor store which specializes in backcountry rather than downhill or cross-country skiing. There are many choices to be made and a number of similar designs: touring, telemark, mountaineering as well as true backcounty skis. Bindings can be the traditional three pin with cable or the NNN-BC (New Nordic Norm Backcountry) style with no cable. Mountaineering type bindings can be used with the heel free for the ascent and locked down on the descent. The key is to have a ski which is strong, has enough flotation for untracked snow and metal edges for hard packed snow, ice, and steep traverses. The ski should be designed to accommodate climbing skins. The bindings must allow the heel to rise up and down and the boots should cover the ankle both for support as well as protection from the snow. Gaiters are worn over the boots in deep snow.

AVALANCHES

In North America, on average, 24 people a year are killed by avalanches. Most of them are backcountry skiers and snowboarders but some are hikers. While not the last word in avalanche avoidance and safety this section should serve as advance notice and a warning to learn all one can about snow and the associated danger before venturing into an area prone to avalanches. The subject does not lend itself to learning from a book as it is an imprecise science involving experience and judgment best learned from an experienced source while in the field.

Avalanches can occur in any season provided the conditions are right. Any slide which releases enough snow to bury you is considered an avalanche: an avalanche path 98 ft (30 m) long has killed and so have slope angles of only 25°. A large percentage of the people caught in avalanches triggered the avalanche themselves. Sometimes the resistance holding the snow in place is only slightly greater than the downward force exerted by the weight of the snow. The extra weight of a person may be all that is required to upset the balance and trigger the avalanche.

Persons who have survived being carried away by avalanches find the experience terrifying. Once caught, the individual is powerless to resist the force of the snow, is overwhelmed, and may be tumbled to the extent that one loses any sense of up or down. The recommended strategy is to use swimming motions in an effort to stay on top of the snow as it is moving. As the snow begins to slow, a hand in front of the face will help to keep snow from lodging up the nose or in the mouth and will create an air space for breathing. If possible the other hand should be thrust upwards towards the snow surface. A hand showing above the snow will lead to more immediate rescue. When the snow stops moving the crystals bind tightly together and the victim may be encased by snow with arms and legs locked in position, the slightest body movements may be impossible. Rescue will depend on the quick action of hiking companions. Death comes from injuries, suffocation, or hypothermia. The survival rate is relatively low and most victims will be dead within the hour. Rescue must occur in the first few minutes.

Typically, avalanche victims have an inadequate understanding of the danger. Safety lies in recognizing avalanche danger and avoiding it. When hiking in mountainous terrain, watch for avalanche and out-of-bound warning signs. In the United States the Forest Service issues their Backcountry Avalanche Forecast; contact (206) 526-6677. In Canada the Canadian Avalanche Centre issues an Avalanche Information Bulletin and can be reached at (604) 290-9333 or 1-800-667-1105. Avalanche danger changes with each change in weather so it is also important to continually update avalanche reports and speak with knowledgeable local people familiar with the terrain you will be encountering.

Most avalanches occur on slopes between 30° and 45° with the most dangerous slope being 38°. Lesser grades tend to be more stable while higher grades tend to regularly slough off snow so that large unstable layers are not as likely to build up. The Silva Ranger compass is equipped with an inclinometer for measuring slope angles.

Gullies and chutes are often the easiest routes for travel but in winter they are the most dangerous because they tend to funnel avalanching snow. Avoid going up or down gullies. Use the ridges

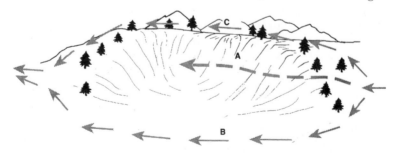

Fig. 15.2: Available routes in order of safety from avalanches: A bad; B better; C best.

to one side of the gully. If snow breaks loose it will be more likely to avalanche down the slope and into a gully.

Avoid crossing gullies or open slopes. Far better to climb above unstable slopes or descend and cross below the slope even if this means a longer route.

Look for snow anchors like rocks and trees which tend to stabilize the snow above them. Select routes through heavy forest rather than open slopes. These areas may block the path of an avalanche and create islands of safety and be a place to escape to if an avalanche begins.

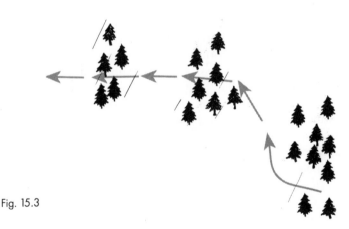

Fig. 15.3

Wind tends to remove snow from slopes standing in its path and deposit it on the sheltered side where wind speed drops. The thickest layers are deposited just over the crest of the slope on the lee side. These thick snow deposits when undercut are called cornices and are particularly unstable. When walking along a ridge, be aware that the part of the ridge you are walking on may be a cornice. The cornice may break. The closer to the edge, the greater the danger. When hiking on snow slopes look up frequently to see what lies above; you may be walking under a cornice or a snow loaded convex slope.

Finally, consider what would happen if there were an avalanche. Where would you be dumped? Would the avalanche push you over a cliff or into a crevasse? Is there a good run out for the snow to spread itself out and dissipate or would the snow be blocked by anchors and pile high?

Fig. 15.4: The wind has carried snow to the lee side of the ridge producing a cornice which endangers both hikers.

If crossing a potentially dangerous slope, cross as high as possible so there is the least amount of unstable slope above you. Cross one person at a time. The second person should go the way the first person went rather than forging a new route. The slope may fail no matter how many people have crossed it but the odds improve if someone has just made it across. If carrying avalanche rescue beacons, use them. Release ski pole wrist straps, unfasten ski safety straps, and undo pack chest and hip straps. If you begin to tumble in an avalanche you do not want encumbrances which will prevent you from righting yourself and staying at the upper surface of the moving snow. On the other hand you will want the zippers of your clothing done up in case you end up in the snow. Watch each person as they cross the slope and if an avalanche hits observe the spot where they were last seen. You will have only minutes to affect a rescue and the last sighting should be the starting point of the search.

COLD INJURIES

The body's extremities can be damaged by low winter temperatures. Blood circulation may be insufficient to keep fingers, toes, or even parts of the face sufficiently warm.

Frost nip is the initial stage of cold damage. The onset is insidious and the person affected may not realize that a patch of skin is starting to freeze and has become numb. Circulation fails and the skin turns white. There may be a tingling sensation or pain at the affected site. Frost nip requires only that the affected skin be rewarmed. If untreated, frost nip will progress to the next stage which is frostbite. Aspirin is useful for all cold tissue injuries and improves blood flow and reduces secondary tissue damage. Consider putting Aspirin in your winter first aid kit.

More serious than frost nip is frostbite. In frostbite, the surface layer has frozen but the tissue beneath has not. Common sites for frostbite are: fingertips, toes, earlobes and the tip of the nose. Anything which restricts blood flow can contribute to cold injuries. Commonly, boots which are too tight will reduce blood circulation to the feet and become a contributing factor for cold and frostbitten feet. In cold weather it is nice to be wearing an extra pair of socks, but the advantage is lost if the extra socks make the boots too tight. Before thawing out the affected body part, consider the result. If the victim has frost-bitten feet but must continue walking to safety, it will be better to delay thawing. Thawed flesh will be more subject to further tissue damage and will refreeze more easily. At the very least, the injury will blister and be extremely painful.

If thawing is to be attempted, do it gently and with care: no rubbing and only moderate heat. Submerse the body part in lukewarm water of about normal body temperature. If too much heat is applied, the tissue will be further damaged. It was once believed that cold injuries should be rubbed with snow and one sometimes reads accounts of this being done. We now know that this practice is incorrect; rubbing an injury or exposing it to unnecessary cold will only make the damage greater.

Remember that frostbite is a danger to limbs but hypothermia is a danger to life. Hypothermia must be treated before frostbite. If the extremities are warmed while the body's core is cold, cardiac arrest may follow. Refer to Chapter 1 for a full discussion of afterdrop.

The step beyond frostbite is a frozen body part. Here the underlying tissue is also frozen. Reheating is best delayed until the victim is in a medical facility. Quite apart from the medical complications arising from the damaged tissue is the pain. The pain will be severe and strong pain control medication will be required.

16.

GOING ALONE

We are often told by loved ones and search and rescue organizations never to hike alone, but there is a definite appeal to being on one's own in the wilderness particularly on overnight trips. It is an opportunity, rarely available anywhere else, to examine our primitive fears and get to know ourselves better.

Derek Stanbury hiked solo across the frozen Great Slave Lake, then soloed Alaska's Mt. McKinley. To be in wild places is to enjoy a sense of freedom — and that freedom is unlimited when hiking alone. Derek says he hikes and climbs alone to avoid compromises, to face a great challenge head-on, the ultimate test of self-reliance. Being alone in the bush is not in itself dangerous — but it is a dramatically different experience than being with others. As Derek would say — there are no compromises.

You go on exactly the hike you want to, starting and stopping at exactly the time you choose. Along the way you go exactly the pace you wish, you eat when you are hungry, you drink when you are thirsty, stop when you are tired and look only at what you wish to. There are no conversations to distract you, no polite chit chat, no consultations or discussions. If you spend your work week on the telephone, in meetings, or dealing with the public, then here is the way to rejuvenate yourself.

The downside to being alone, of course, is that when things go wrong, you are on your own and the panic will be greater. If you hurt yourself there is no one to go for help.

No matter how complicated your life may be — alone in the bush life becomes very simple. Eat, stay warm and dry and don't get lost. You are free of other considerations.

Whether alone or with a group, traveling in the wilderness is one of life's pure and simple pleasures. Be healthy, be happy and above all, be prepared. To fully enjoy the experience one requires the bush basics; the ability to find one's way, and to remain comfortable. With these and a healthy dose of common-sense, being away from home in the backcountry is a refuge, a tonic, and a balm for the soul.

SOURCES

Canada. *Biting Flies Attacking Man and Livestock in Canada.*
Agriculture Canada, 1985.

Canada. *Black Flies.* Agriculture Canada, 1973.

Auerbach, M.D. *Medicine for the Outdoors, A Guide to Emergency
Medical Procedures and First Aid.* New York, Little Brown and Co.,
1986.

Barbour, Alan G., M.D. *Lyme Disease, the Cause, the Cure, the
Controversy.* Johns Hopkins University Press, 1996.

Belton, Peter. *The Mosquitoes of British Columbia.* British Columbia
Provincial Museum, 1983.

Gillett, J.D. *The Mosquito.* Doubleday and Company Inc., 1972.

Hearne, Samuel. *A Journey from Prince of Wales Fort in Hudson's
Bay to the Northern Ocean.* M.G. Hurtig Ltd., 1971.

Herrero, Stephen. *Bear Attacks Their Causes and Avoidance.* Lyons
and Burford, 1985.

Klots, Alexander and Elsie. *Insects of North America.* Doubleday and Company Inc., 1976.

Klutschak, Heinrich. *Overland to Starvation Cove, with the Inuit in Search of Franklin 1878 — 1880* translated by William Barr. University of Toronto Press, 1987.

Maniguet, Xavier. *Survival: How to Prevail in a Hostile Environment.* Facts on File Inc., 1988.

British Columbia. *Safety Guide to Cougars.* Ministry of Environment, QP#96387.

British Columbia. *Cougars of British Columbia.* Ministry of Environment, QP#81193.

British Columbia. *Fundamentals of Fire Fighting.* Ministry of Forests, 1992 and 1994.

Northwest Territories. *Safety in Bear Country, 2nd edition.* Department of Renewable Resources, 1992.

Peterson, Lester. *The Cape Scott Story.* Sunfire Publications, 1974.

Rawicz, Slavomir. *The Long Walk.* Harper and Row, 1956.

Shanks, Bernard. *Wilderness Survival.* Universe Books, 1980.

Syrotuck, William G. *Analysis of Lost Person Behavior.* Arner Publications, Inc., 1976.

Whitman, Walt. *Leaves of Grass.* The New American Library, 1964.

Wood, D.M.; Dang, P.T.; Ellis, R.A. *The Insects and Arachnids of Canada, Part 6 — The Mosquitoes of Canada Diptera: Culcidiae.* Agriculture Canada, 1979.

RECOMMENDED READING

Barbour, Alan G, M.D. *Lyme Disease, the Cause, the Cure, the Controversy.* Johns Hopkins University Press, 1996. This book probably contains everything you really want to know about Lyme disease.

Daffern, Tony. *Avalanche Safety for Skiers and Climbers, 2nd edition.* Rocky Mountain Books, Calgary, 1992. If it were possible to become an expert in avalanches by reading a book, this would be the one.

First Aid, Quick Information for Mountaineering and Backcountry Use. Mountaineers, Seattle, 1995. This 36 page pamphlet is not a substitute for a formal first aid course but it is handy in a first aid kit. It covers the basics but not CPR (cardio pulmonary resuscitation).

Grey Owl. *The Men of the Last Frontier.* Stoddart Publishing Co. Ltd., 1931. This is one of several books written by an Englishman who adopted an Indian name and lived the life of a trapper. He saw and recorded a time when natives still lived on the land and men like himself roamed unmapped wilderness.

Jacobsen, Cliff. *Canoeing Wild Rivers, 2nd edition.* ICS Books, Indiana, 1989. For those who already have paddling skills and wish to paddle wild and remote northern rivers.

London, Jack. *To Build a Fire.* Century Magazine, 1908. A classic short story. It recounts the tale of a hiker traveling at extremely low temperatures and his desperate but failed attempt to light a fire.

Graydon, Don, ed. *Mountaineering: The Freedom of the Hills, 5th edition.* The Mountaineers, 1992. The classic textbook on mountaineering.

Shelton, James Gary. *Bear Encounter Survival Guide.* Self-published, 1994. A disturbing book. Jim presents evidence to show that present attitudes and policies towards bears and bear management are dangerously wrong.

Hiking guidebooks. If you can't find a guidebook for the trail you are interested in, look up "hiking" in Books in Print at your local library. This reference source lists title, author, publisher and price.

Meyer, Kathleen. *How to Shit in the Woods, 2nd edition.* Ten Speed Press, 1994. An entertaining book about a taboo subject.

Rawicz, Slavomir. *The Long Walk.* Harper and Row, 1956. So extreme you may not believe it. Rawicz escaped the Soviet Gulag entirely on foot, crossing Siberia in winter, the Gobi Desert, and the Himalayas, before seeking refuge in India.

Index